A CHICKEN SOUP FOR THE SOUL

Christmas

*Stories to Warm Your Heart and
Share with Family During the Holidays*

Jack Canfield
Mark Victor Hansen

Health Communications, Inc.
Deerfield Beach, Florida

www.hcibooks.com
www.chickensoup.com

We would like to acknowledge the following publishers and individuals for permission to reprint the following material.

Christmas of My Dreams. Reprinted by permission of Cheryl Kirking Kilker. ©1994 Cheryl Kirking Kilker.

Cheap Sax. Reprinted by permission of Robin Lee Shope. ©2007 Robin Lee Shope.

A Closed Highway Opened Hearts. Reprinted by permission of Martha Jane Ajango. ©2006 Martha Jane Ajango.

In Touch with My Inner Elf. Reprinted by permission of Loree Jean Gold. ©2003 Loree Jean Gold.

It's the Simple Things. Reprinted by permission of Nancy J. Kopp. ©2006 Nancy J. Kopp.

(Continued on page 265)

Library of Congress Cataloging-in-Publication Data

A chicken soup for the soul Christmas / [compiled by] Jack Canfield, Mark Victor Hansen.
    p. cm.

ISBN-13: 978-0-7573-0646-4 (trade paper)
ISBN-10: 0-7573-0646-2 (trade paper)
    1. Christmas—Miscellanea. I. Canfield, Jack, 1944– II. Hansen, Mark Victor.

BV45.C537 2007
242'.335—dc22

2007014816

Publisher: Health Communications, Inc.
        3201 S.W. 15th Street
        Deerfield Beach, FL 33442-8190

Cover design by Andrea Perrine Brower
Interior formatting by Lawna Patterson Oldfield

Contents

1. The Meaning of Christmas

2. Through the Eyes of a Child

Acknowledgments

We wish to express our heartfelt gratitude to the following people who helped make this book possible.

Our families, who have been chicken soup for our souls!

Jack's family: Inga, Travis, Riley, Christopher, Oran, and Kyle, for all their love and support.

Mark's family: Patty, Elisabeth, and Melanie Hansen, for once again sharing and lovingly supporting us in creating yet another book.

Our publisher, Peter Vegso, for his vision and commitment to bringing *Chicken Soup for the Soul* to the world.

Patty Aubery and Russ Kalmaski, for being there on every step of the journey, with love, laughter, and endless creativity.

Barbara Lomonaco, for nourishing us with truly wonderful stories and cartoons.

D'ette Corona, for being there to answer any questions along the way.

Patty Hansen, for her thorough and competent handling of the legal and licensing aspects of the *Chicken Soup for the Soul* books. You are magnificent at the challenge!

Veronica Romero, Teresa Collette, Robin Yerian, Jesse Ianniello, Lauren Edelstein, Lisa Williams, Laurie Hartman, Patti Clement, Meagan Romanello, Noelle Champagne, Jody Emme, Debbie Lefever, Michelle Adams, Dee Dee

Romanello, Shanna Vieyra, and Gina Romanello, who support Jack's and Mark's businesses with skill and love.

Patricia Brady, for editing the final manuscript. As always, you are a pleasure to work with.

Michele Matriscini, Carol Rosenberg, Andrea Gold, Allison Janse, Katheline St. Fort, our editors at Health Communications, Inc., for their devotion to excellence.

Terry Burke, Tom Sand, Lori Golden, Kelly Johnson Maragni, Karen Bailiff Ornstein, Patricia McConnell, Kim Weiss, Paola Fernandez-Rana, the marketing, sales, and PR departments at Health Communications, Inc., for doing such an incredible job supporting our books.

Tom Sand, Claude Choquette, and Luc Jutras, who manage year after year to get our books transferred into thirty-six languages around the world.

The art department at Health Communications, Inc., for their talent, creativity, and unrelenting patience in producing book covers and inside designs that capture the essence of Chicken Soup: Larissa Hise Henoch, Lawna Patterson Oldfield, Andrea Perrine Brower, Anthony Clausi, and Dawn Von Strolley Grove.

Our glorious panel of readers, who helped us make the final selections and made invaluable suggestions on how to improve the book.

To everyone who submitted a story, we deeply appreciate your letting us into your lives and sharing your experiences with us. For those whose stories were not chosen for publication, we hope the stories you are about to enjoy convey what was in your heart.

Because of the size of this project, we may have left out the names of some people who contributed along the way. If so, we are sorry, but please know that we really do appreciate you very much.

We are truly grateful and love you all!

Introduction

Remember when our eyes lit up with excited anticipation as our parents took the Christmas tree lights out of storage? These were not the small, delicate lights we see today, but the enamel-coated bulbs that eventually moved outdoors to decorate the front yard. December always made our souls sing with glee, while the snowy month softened the edges from even our strictest teachers. Some of our traditional friends celebrated St. Nicholas Day by placing a shoe outside their bedroom door—only to find candy in it the next morning! But the enviable kids owned the ultimate Christmas countdown device: the Advent Calendar. These glitter-sprinkled thin cardboard sheets contained tiny numbered windows that opened from December first through Christmas Eve. All twenty-four windows contained some illustrated symbol of the holiday—the largest window containing the manger of Jesus. The bigger the family, the more competition to open the last window on December twenty-fourth!

We also remember some of the hard, challenging times when we needed to look beyond our painful moment and use resilient hearts to restore the joy of the holiday. Difficult as the season was, we still remember it with empathy and give to others who later walk in the same footsteps.

This is Christmas at its best and most traditional flavor. Through the years, we've welcomed our friends and neighbors of different religions and ethnicities to come and help us celebrate our traditions—and, in the process, learned their holidays in many ways were not as different as our own! The meaning is the same. While we knew each other's differences, we also accepted our friends' cultures and customs as symbols of their love. It's understandable why our eccentric neighbors down the road want to keep their Christmas tree up all year long—the feeling of happiness and hope needs to live through 365 days. Perhaps we should all keep up our own special "tree" of joy throughout the year, whether it's one decorated with big bulbs to remind us of our blessed childhood, or one decorated with small, delicate lights that show us that the gifts and privileges we now possess are truly a miracle from a divine power that everyone can share. We hope the enclosed stories are shared with family and friends during the holidays.

Share with Us

We would like to invite you to send us stories you would like to see published in future editions of *Chicken Soup for the Soul*.

We would also love to hear your reactions to the stories in this book. Please let us know what your favorite stories are and how they affected you.

Please submit your stories on our website:

www.chickensoup.com

Chicken Soup for the Soul
PO Box 30880
Santa Barbara, CA 93130
fax: 805-563-2945

We hope you enjoy reading this book as much as we enjoyed compling, editing, and writing it.

1

THE MEANING OF CHRISTMAS

Oh, Christmas isn't just a day. It's a frame of mind . . . and that's what's been changing. That's why I'm glad I'm here. Maybe I can do something about it.

Kris Kringle, Miracle on 34th Street

Christmas of My Dreams

The Christmas cookies are all frosted,
the gingerbread men have purple hair,
And 'cause little hands can only reach so high,
the top half of the tree is quite bare!
But the bottom half sparkles with tinsel,
and foil stars and paper chains,
And along with the gifts the Wise Men bring
are three nickels and two candy canes.

Although it's true our money's tighter than ever,
our love just keeps on growing, it seems,
And I couldn't ask for anything more,
this is the Christmas of my dreams.

I used to have such great expectations
about Christmas and just how it should be,
With the picture-perfect table of goodies
and lots of presents under the tree.
Although I still love the tinsel and glitter,
the scent of pine and songs in the air,
When all's said and done, what matters most
is the Christmas love that all of us share.

Although our Christmas may not be very fancy,
like the ones you see in magazines,
I wouldn't trade it for anything,
this is the Christmas of my dreams.

So let's each count our blessings,
and thank our God above,
As we celebrate this season
of the greatest gift of love.
Our Christmas may not be very fancy,
like the ones you see in magazines,
But I couldn't ask for anything more,
this is the Christmas of my dreams.

Cheryl Kirking

Cheap Sax

*We can only be said to be alive
in those moments when our hearts are
conscious of our treasures.*

Thornton Wilder

I attend garage sales on weekends. It's called therapy—
my respite from teaching middle school five days a week.
I allot myself forty dollars when I foray into yard-sale
heaven. Always loaded with hope, I salivate to find something I can turn a good profit on by selling it on eBay. I'm
princess la-de-da. Just weeks before Christmas, I found an
ad in the classifieds for an inside moving sale. My dear husband cautioned me to be extra careful with my choices.
After all, our daughter's college loan was due, and it was
the season of gift giving. Extra money would sure come in
handy right now, and we couldn't afford to waste a penny.

Cold rain hammered down on my car and turned narrow
streets into icy waterways. The windshield wipers couldn't
keep up with the downpour, making it hard to see anything
beyond the front of my car. This was good because the
weather was apt to keep my competitors home today. I was

like Santa when it came to garage sales—no storm or cold of winter could keep me from my appointed rounds.

I parked right in front of the house. The front door was open as if to say, "Come in, come in, and buy my treasures." Blessed me, I was the second person to cross the threshold. Under a pile of old bedspreads in the back bedroom, I opened a case and found a shiny saxophone. It had a beautiful engraving of a woman on it, and I soon learned it was not only vintage but in pristine condition to boot. It was mine for twenty dollars.

Not familiar with the value of instruments, I called my husband to do a quick search on eBay to find out what they were going for. No way could I afford to make a financial mistake and end up with another white elephant to store in my shed. It was crowded enough in there as it was.

"Why are you calling me on your cell phone? We are out of minutes, so this call is expensive," Rick complained.

"Just look, please."

A sigh. Over the phone, I could hear his fingers running over the keyboard, then silence. "There aren't any listed." Odd. It seemed to me that someone should have at least one saxophone for sale.

"Are you sure about this?" I asked, while adding up our minutes and multiplying each by one dollar.

"Not one."

Trying to save money, I closed the call without saying good-bye. Now I worried. For twenty dollars, I now owned a shiny saxophone that might not sell at all. What did I know about musical instruments anyway? The only thing I could play was the radio. On my way out of the house, an elderly man stopped me and asked if I would sell him the sax. He would pay me twenty dollars more than what I paid. I would not only get my twenty dollars back, but also make twenty dollars on it within minutes of my purchase. It sounded good to me, and I viewed it as

God's unexpected provision, a Christmas blessing.

The man and I stepped outside to find a dry spot under the overhang of the house and struck our deal. He opened his worn wallet and shuffled through the one-dollar bills searching for larger bills. With shaking fingers, he pulled out one crisp twenty and then another and handed them to me. Then he pulled the sax in its case from my arms.

I chuckled, leaping over rain puddles on the way back to my car, thinking about how pleased my husband would be with me that I had turned a profit so quickly. With temperatures quickly falling, there weren't any other sales, so I returned home a bit richer than when I had left.

"Look at you!" Rick said proudly as I handed him the cash.

Then I sat at the computer, went to the eBay home page, and typed in the brand of saxophone I had owned for less than five minutes. To my horror, three exact matches came up—and they were all selling for over five hundred dollars with days left on the auctions. "Rick!" I yelled, pointing at the screen. "Look!"

My dear husband wrinkled his nose and said, "Oh."

"You said there weren't any saxophones listed!" I became weak. I was losing consciousness.

"Hmmm, that's weird. When I looked, there weren't any listed."

Suddenly, I realized what he had done. Rick hadn't gone to the eBay home page. He had gone to my seller's page, and, of course, I didn't have a sax listed. I had an enamel coffee pot with no bids, a sunbonnet girl quilt with no bids, and a primitive cabinet, also without a bid. I had sold the sax cheap. God wanted to bless me abundantly, and I had blown it! It was as if someone had snatched money right out of my pocket, and I had just let it happen.

Frantic, my first instinct was to drive around town, try to find the man who bought the sax, and offer him sixty dollars to let me buy it back. He would get his forty dollars back and make twenty on it, just as I had done. It sounded reasonable to me, but with the wind now reaching forty miles an hour and sleet large enough to cause tree limbs to fall, I figured I better stay home. But I did put the saxophone auctions on my watch page and groaned loudly with every bid. At the end of one auction, with a final bid of nearly a thousand dollars, I shrieked, "That coulda been *me!*"

With Christmas a few days away, I couldn't shake the negative frame of mind I allowed myself to sink into. Running my fingers through my hair, I lamented over working so hard for every penny I earned. Couldn't I just catch a break one time? I was at my job for at least ten hours a day, teaching and then tutoring both before and after school. On weekends, I was so worn out that I spent the whole time sleeping. Even with my husband's overtime, our monthly budget was stretched to the max. The extra cash would have been such a luxury. My blessing had been stolen.

But it was done, over. No turning back the day for a do-over. Yet, I just couldn't let it go. Late at night, I sat by the lighted Christmas tree feeling quite angry with myself for harboring ill feelings. My brain kept replaying over and over that moment of selling the sax. My therapy was supposed to relieve tension, not create it. I felt envious and filled with greed. God was revealing a side of me that I had no idea was there, but this situation sure shined a spotlight on it.

I opened the Bible to Galatians 6:9 (NIV): "Let us not become weary in doing good, for at the proper time we will reap a harvest if we do not give up." Next I turned in my concordance to the verses on praising God and made note cards of ten verses. Each time I thought about the sax, I lifted my arms upward and praised God, thanking him, and quoting scripture. "Give thanks in all circumstances, for this is God's will for you in Christ Jesus" (1 Thess. 5:18 NIV). It was amazing how the turmoil fled, leaving behind pure happiness. It set me totally free, and once more my life became enjoyable. I also let my husband off the hook, and his life became enjoyable once again, too.

Our family had a blessed Christmas. We attended church together, had a big feast, and everyone found what they wished for under the tree. But my son's gift to me took the prize for the holiday. Inside the box was forty dollars worth of one-dollar bills—the perfect denomination for garage sales. A few months later, this gift came in handy when garage sales were aplenty once again due to good weather.

One morning, at one such sale, I spied my sax buyer hunched over a box, going through old sheet music! A twinge of regret hit me, so I pretended I didn't see him. But he recognized me and called out, "Hello there! Have you found any treasures today?"

"No," I heaved out the word heavily, then sang inside my spirit, *Praise him, praise him, Jesus our precious redeemer. . . .*

As I turned to walk away, he grabbed hold of my arm. "I want you to know that because of your spontaneous generosity, I found my old passion and took up the sax again. Being retired, I now volunteer my time to teach kids how to play it." He wiggled his fingers over the throat of an invisible sax. It was then that I noticed his frailty, his worn clothes, and his old shoes.

My perspective totally shifted. I thought he had taken my blessing, when in fact he was my blessing. God's provision is for all of us. And I was blessed to have found it twice in the most unusual place. I call that a double blessing.

Robin Lee Shope

A Closed Highway Opened Hearts

*The everyday kindness of the
back roads more than make up for the
acts of greed in the headlines.*

Charles Kuralt

Several years ago, our family of five began its annual Christmas trek to Grandma's house. As we traveled from Wisconsin to Indiana on Christmas Eve day, the weather became increasingly worse. Heavy snow continued to fall, and high winds, which swept across the flat farmlands, whipped up the snow and dumped it into drifts across the highway, slowing traffic to a crawl. All movement came to a complete halt near an off-ramp when we encountered snowplows parked sideways across the road to block the highway. Their bundled-up operators, who stood beside the plows in the road, slogged to our car to inform us, "The highway's closed. This is as far as you can go."

"But what can we do?" we asked.

They replied, "There is a small church just down the road. They have opened its doors to stranded travelers." Creeping carefully down the off-ramp, we caught sight of a white wooden building with a spire that became our inn for Christmas Eve night.

We entered the church and discovered a couple of hundred fellow travelers who had taken shelter. The refugees ran the gamut in age from babies to old folks, representing all humanity. Even a few dogs huddled next to their masters. The church's young pastor evidently started a calling chain among his parishioners, asking for their help. They responded quickly by braving the bitter cold and deep snow to bring us blankets, pillows, cookies, and cakes. Then a contingent stayed on to turn the fellowship hall into an impromptu restaurant by preparing hot chili, cocoa, and coffee for their disconsolate guests.

We sat around in small groups, disappointed that our anticipated plans with our loved ones had been ruined. As there were no cell phones in those days, there was a continuous long line of people impatiently waiting to use the church's wall phone to alert relatives to their safety, to tell them where they were, and that they would not be getting home for Christmas.

Our daughter Deb brought her guitar with her. She took it out of its case and, while sitting on the gym floor, began to softly sing Christmas carols. Soon, a small group gathered around to join their voices with hers. They were to become "our group" for the rest of the time. Deb played quietly far into the night, as people began to seek out pews, hallways, or floors on which to sleep. The young minister and his wife stayed at the church with us all night. When Christmas morning dawned, he led our rumpled, dispossessed group in our own private worship service.

As the sun announced the arrival of the new day, a different batch of church members left their own Christmas preparations and plodded through the snow, bringing pancake mix, juice, and eggs to make us breakfast. Many of the dispirited visitors' thoughts traveled to the destination their bodies could not reach, and they envisioned blazing Christmas trees surrounded by piles of unopened presents. Since our new acquaintances replaced the families we could not be with, we spent the morning comparing stories. When noontime found us still snowbound, a second crew arrived to fix lunch. A mechanic left his warm home and family to work outside in the zero weather, jumping cars that had frozen overnight. A filling station owner interrupted his Christmas celebration to open his station so we could have gas in our tanks in case the roads became passable.

Late in the afternoon, word arrived that one lane of a road had been cleared, so our family decided to try completing the journey to Indianapolis. After a harrowing six-hour drive on slippery roads, we arrived at our grandparents' home late Christmas night. Although it was not the holiday we had planned, we all knew it was one we would remember when all the other ones were forgotten. We received a gift that could not fit under a tree, wrapped in the caring compassion of those church members. They put aside their own comfort and traditions to welcome us at their "inn," not just with food, but with cheer and loving concern. We witnessed the true spirit of Christmas, of giving instead of receiving, by a congregation who set their own celebrations and enjoyment aside to care for strangers in their tiny town of Morocco, Indiana.

Martha Ajango

In Touch with My Inner Elf

It was three weeks before Christmas, and my life looked pretty bleak. I was cold. I was broke. And I was worried. My small film production company was on its deathbed. My business partner left for Berlin to visit her lover. Everyone was shopping and leaving for the holidays. But I had big plans, too. No, I wasn't traveling back to New York or visiting my parents in Florida. I was going to stay in Nashville, go to my office every day, stare at the phone that never rang, and feel tremendously sorry for myself. I mean, did I really have any other choice?

One morning, I was pacing in front of my desk, scanning through the newspaper, and right in front of my face was a help-wanted ad. UPS needed Santa's helpers to sit in the little jump seat next to the driver. When the driver made a delivery stop, the Santa's helper would deliver a package. This appealed to me. It seemed like an interesting job. It wouldn't be overwhelming. It would be Zen-like, nice and simple. When there were no more packages, and the back of the truck was empty, the workday would be over. It would be a gig that was totally different from my usual job. I wouldn't have to be creative. I wouldn't have to deal with crazy clients. I wouldn't have to fulfill a million responsibilities. All I had to do was lift a maximum of sixty-five pounds, run up to someone's front door, and deliver Christmas packages to people who would be smiling and anticipating my arrival with joy. Plus, I'd make $9.50 an hour.

That morning I drove to UPS to apply for the gig. I could hardly contain my excitement. I walked in, dressed from head to toe in black Italian designer wear. The woman at the desk looked at me quizzically. I told her I was applying for a Santa's helper position. She asked me if I was sure and looked at me like I was crazy. I told her I was never more certain of anything in my entire life. I told her about my company, how it was on the verge of bankruptcy. I told her that my business partner was in Berlin with her lover. I told her I was forty-five-and-a-half, but I could easily lift sixty-five pounds, and I pushed up my sleeve and flexed my biceps. I explained to her how much I needed this job at this moment in my life, that this was more than a job to me—it was the key to my sanity. I put aside my pride and dignity, and I begged her to please let me work as a Santa's helper. When I finished my plea, she was practically in tears. Then she smiled at me and said those three magical words: "Welcome to UPS!" I immediately got fitted for my uniform. Even though I would have preferred that the jacket and pants were more fitted, and I knew that brown was definitely not my color, I felt like a million bucks.

Bright and early the next morning, I was riding shotgun in a huge UPS truck filled with 175 packages. Arthur was at the wheel. He had worked with UPS for over eighteen years. Arthur never thought he'd be a UPS driver. He studied art history in college, and his specialty was the Italian Renaissance era. He became a university professor for several years and then discovered he could make more money driving a UPS truck. In between deliveries, Arthur and I talked about literature, art, opera, and PBS. His route took us through rural areas and housing developments where all the modest two-story red-bricked houses looked alike.

That first day, I jumped in and out of the truck over one hundred times for over twelve hours. When I got home, I collapsed. I couldn't remember ever working so hard or ever feeling so sore. I drifted into a deep sleep, wondering if I would be able to get up and do it all over again the next day.

Somehow, I did. I got up day after day, and by the end of the week, it got easier.

Dogs would chase us, and sometimes Arthur threatened them with the big stick he kept in the back. But for the most part, people greeted us with big smiles and open arms. I was totally into being the "UPS Lady." People knew if I knocked at their door that I came bearing gifts. I brought people happiness. And that was enough to make me happy, too.

My second week, I was split up between two drivers. In the mornings I rode with Pete through the blue-collar, working-class neighborhoods. Pete had just turned twenty-six. I looked at him and thought, *My God, I could be his mother!* He was polite and protective and kept calling me "Ma'am," which irritated me. When he started to treat me like his mother and took an eighty-five-pound package out of my hands, that's when I'd had enough. I had to put a stop to it for my own self-respect and in the name of sisterhood. I needed to prove to him I wasn't some middle-aged wimp, so I grabbed that eighty-five-pound package right out of his twenty-six-year-old hands, whisked it off, and delivered it, shattering Pete's stereotype about women being weak and helpless. After we'd cleared up this issue, every morning between deliveries, he'd talk, I'd listen, and then he'd ask me for advice. Pete would actually turn off his heavy metal music and listen closely to me, like I was some wise, old sage.

During my last week, TJ was at the wheel. Having been a UPS driver for over twenty-two years, TJ had seniority and therefore drove the best route—the most beautiful areas and upscale neighborhoods in Nashville. We'd enter private roads and driveways with no-trespassing signs and find ourselves on incredible estates with acres and acres of rolling hills dotted with running horses. Or we'd drive up one of those mysterious, long, and winding private driveways that led up to the top of a mountain, and there would stand a tremendous home that was right out of the pages of *Architectural Digest,* built from imported wood and custom-tinted glass, with Italian marble floors and an Olympic-sized swimming pool in the middle of the foyer. I was a tourist in a town where I had lived for thirteen years, discovering places I'd never known existed. I felt like I was traveling in a foreign country, seeing things for the first time, with all my senses geared up—taking it all in. Every day I was in awe of the beauty, in awe of the moment. For the first time in a long time, I was living life in the present tense and enjoying what it had to offer. And TJ was my fellow companion and travel guide.

TJ was a year younger than me. He told me his wife didn't understand him and that he adored his two precious little daughters. He beamed when he showed me the photo of two beautiful little blonde girls smiling at the camera. As we drove along the black-posted fence of a picture-perfect Tennessee walking horse farm, TJ told me horrifying stories of his time spent in Vietnam. There was the army buddy who died in his arms, the villages he helped burn down, and the innocent women and children he saw die. And now, after all of these years, his nightmares kept recurring. He planned to retire in a few years and move to Florida because it was always sunny, and he wanted to show his girls the ocean. By the end of my last UPS week, TJ and I had become old friends. We'd talk and reminisce about a lot of things that happened in our lifetime—Vietnam, Woodstock, the assassination of President Kennedy, Janis Joplin, and Jimi Hendrix.

On my last day, TJ and the other drivers bought me lunch at Captain Dee's. The parking lot was filled with UPS trucks. I was the only woman, the only Yankee, and the only Jew—yet we had bonded, me and the boys in brown.

TJ and I worked late that night. It was Christmas Eve, and we finished delivering the last of 223 packages. Our final stop was The Loveless Café, a funky but famous fried-chicken-with-biscuits-'n'-gravy restaurant out in the middle of nowhere. Right beside The Loveless Café was a small white trailer. An old, beat-up plaid couch with springs poking out rested on a pile of weeds, next to an old rusty washing machine. Inside, the trailer was filled with boxes and boxes of Loveless Café's blackberry and strawberry jams, peach preserves, and country hams that had to be shipped out before Christmas. TJ and I loaded the boxes onto the truck in silence. There was sadness in the silence—the sadness that comes with saying good-bye. The day was over. TJ closed the back doors of the truck and went back inside the trailer to get the paper-work signed. I waited outside. I stood on the porch of that trailer and watched the most glorious red and gold sunset spill over The Loveless Café—and me and my brown UPS uniform. And, at that moment, I knew that whatever was next, whatever lay ahead, I was going to get through it just fine. Santa's helper couldn't have asked for a better gift than that.

Loree Gold

It's the Simple Things

Ken and I have been a host family for Czech exchange students who come to study at Kansas State University for the past six or seven years. The students live on their own, but we are there to answer questions, show them around town when they arrive, and invite them to our home for dinner now and then. They lead busy lives, but we e-mail or phone to keep in touch.

This year, we have two young women who are both majoring in the study of architecture. Jana and Klara attend university in Prague, but both come from smaller towns in the Czech Republic. They arrived in the United States the day after new airline regulations regarding what can be carried on and what must be checked went into effect. The day before they left home, their luggage had to be sorted out and rearranged to meet the new regulations. Then there was a paperwork snafu in New York when they went through immigration and customs. Before they knew what had happened, they were taken to a tiny room filled to overflowing with other immigrants who had problems of one kind or another. Most of the people in there were from Asian countries or the Arab world. These two tall, blonde girls huddled together in a corner, expecting the worst. Finally, the paperwork got sorted out, and they had to find a new flight to Kansas City since they'd missed their connecting flight with the delay. The customs officials in New York refused to help them, so they marched off to find the counter for their airline and managed to get on another flight with the help of a kind and helpful ticket agent.

Meanwhile, we knew only that they had not arrived as originally scheduled. Once they knew what flight they would be on, they did call, and a full twenty-four hours beyond the expected time, they arrived at our door—desperately tired, longing for a shower, and hungry after traveling nearly two full days and nights. They spent their first week with us in our home while looking for housing and getting registered on campus. We spent the time getting to know each other, and taking them to meetings and testing places on campus, as well as orienting them to our community. At the end of the week, they had found a little house to rent with two other Czech students and were ready to begin the semester's classes.

That hot August week seems so long ago. In early December, I invited Klara and Jana and their two housemates to come to dinner to celebrate Christmas. Most of the exchange students travel around the United States during the holiday break, so we try to provide an evening of Christmas cheer for them each year, as it is often the only Christmas celebration they will have. It is heartwarming to watch the wonder and joy on their faces when they walk into our home and see the decorated tree and other Christmas symbols throughout the house. We have a special meal and linger at the table to talk about Christmas traditions in their country and ours. I placed a candy cane above each dinner plate, and this year's group was as surprised as all the others in years past. Candy canes are not known in the Czech Republic, and the

students like them. I guess it is because they are something different. "What do they taste like?" they usually
ask. Try to describe "peppermint" sometime . . . it's not
easy! One of the young men said he was going to Wal-
Mart to buy many candy canes to send home to Prague
for Christmas.

Turns out it's the simple things that mean something to
these young people far from their families and their own
country—a home-cooked meal, conversation, knowing
someone cares about them, and maybe having a candy
cane for the first time. For Ken and me, it's another simple
thing: we end up receiving far more than we give with all
of the students we've had. Not every Christmas gift comes
in a box with wrapping paper and a bow.

Nancy Julien Kopp

The First Christmas

This was my first Christmas alone. I had known it would be difficult, but I had no idea that it was going to be this hard. John had died in September, on the twenty-fifth in fact, so Christmas was three months to the day since his death. I tried hard not to feel sorry for myself but was only successful part of the time.

I learned to play bridge, bought tickets to the symphony, and enrolled in a weekly watercolor class. These things helped pass the time, it was true, but in many ways I felt like I was just going through the motions. I had dreaded the last day of November, knowing that when I tore off the calendar page on the thirtieth it would mean that Christmas was just around the corner, and it would be the first one in forty-six years without my beloved Johnny.

I heaved myself out of the La-Z-Boy with a deep sigh. No sense dwelling on it. I had to stop feeling sorry for myself. Thank the Lord, my daughter Wendy still lived in town, although she had been talking more and more about moving out east since her divorce from Dave. She felt there were more job opportunities in the advertising field out there. Wendy was a go-getter, all right. I could have predicted that she wouldn't stay in Swan River for long, even if her marriage to Dave had worked out. Well, she was here in town for the time being anyway, and at least we'd have each other's company for Christmas dinner.

With that thought in mind, I propelled myself toward the kitchen where the turkey lolled nakedly in the roaster, ready for stuffing. I'd make the stuffing, peel the potatoes, and start on the pie crust. Wendy was making candied yams and some new recipe for blood pudding, of all things! John would have hated it. Truth to tell, so would I. But, sweet man that he was, John would have eaten it anyway, grinning all the while so as not to hurt Wendy's feelings. Such a kind heart. A prince among men. Oh, how I missed him!

A shrill ring startled me from my melancholy reverie. Quickly, I wiped my hands on my apron and reached for the phone. It was Wendy.

"Hi, Mom," my daughter said breathlessly. "I'm on the run here, so I won't keep you. I just want to know whether you'd mind it terribly if we had a couple of guests—some friends of mine. I know it's short notice, but you always cook enough for an army anyway, and I know you'll enjoy meeting them. So, how about it? Is it okay?"

I suddenly felt so tired. I really didn't want to entertain strangers. Just getting through the day was a monumental effort by itself. Reluctantly, I agreed, but Wendy, a sensitive girl from the time she was a child, knew that I didn't mean it. Despite that fact, Wendy rolled along enthusiastically.

"Great then, Mom. I'll pick them up on my way over. See you at six o'clock."

The line went dead before I could ask my daughter exactly who she was bringing, much less say good-bye. Well, it didn't much matter, I supposed. I would put on a brave face and soldier through it.

The rest of the day flew by, it seemed. There was so

much for me to do, what with the cooking, the baking, arranging the centerpiece, and getting the table set. Then I still had myself to get ready—no small task these days. Wendy was always telling me that I was still an attractive woman, and that any man would be thrilled to be seen in my company. She was such a flatterer, that one. No wonder she was successful in advertising!

The doorbell chimed at precisely six o'clock. I could always count on Wendy's being on time. She had gotten that from her father. John hated being late for anything. Putting on a wide smile, I bustled to the door and opened it to my company. Wendy appeared to be alone. Puzzled, I peered out into the clear, wintry night but could not see anyone else on the porch. Suddenly, I heard giggling, and then in the next instant, I felt two sets of woolly arms around me, familiar and comforting.

"How are ya' doing, Clairey-Clairey-quite contrary?" one voice trilled. "Good to see ya, luv."

"Give us a kiss then, ey? Show us you're glad to see us," the other one boomed.

My throat tightened; I felt the tears well up, then spill hotly down my cheeks. I was speechless. Joy and disbelief flooded through me simultaneously. Teddy and Mary-Rose were throwing their suitcases into the front hall in a noisy jumble, both speaking to me at the same time and tugging on my sleeve as they vied for my attention, just as they had when they were children. In a boisterous hodge-podge, Wendy squeezed her aunt and uncle through the narrow entryway, picking up the suitcases, and setting them aside out of the way. Her beaming face, flushed from the cold, creased in a radiant smile.

"All the way from England, and not so much as a 'how d'ya do'!" Teddy teased. "What do you think we should do, Mary-Rose? Maybe we should just turn around and get the next plane for Manchester, ey?"

At last, I found my voice. I had last seen my brother and sister, fraternal twins four years my junior, when I'd gone back home to bury our dear mother. That was thirteen years ago. Of course, they had written, and there was the occasional long-distance phone call, but it was not the same as seeing them. Then, when John had died, they had sent a long, heartfelt telegram and apologized that they could not be with me. Despite my disappointment, I had understood. Manchester was far away; they had their jobs and their families, after all, and it would have cost the Earth to get to Swan River on time for the funeral. And now, incredibly, here they were. Thank the Lord, here they were! With my eyes brimming over, I untangled myself from my siblings' arms and moved over to Wendy, who was standing quietly near the staircase that led upstairs, watching the happy reunion unfolding in front of her.

"Wendy, dear girl of mine, did you orchestrate all of this?" I whispered.

"No big deal, Mom," Wendy replied.

"Oh, my sweet girl, it's a very, very big deal, and I thank you from the bottom of my heart. Now, did you bring along that delicious blood pudding you said you were going to prepare? I can't wait to try it. I'll bet your dad would have loved it!"

Sharon Melnicer

The Christmas Doll

It was the afternoon before Christmas Eve as I stared blearily at my youngest daughter's list. Major dental surgery two days earlier had left me swollen, in pain, and most definitely *not* in the holiday spirit.

To make matters worse, a certain creative young lady had provided me with the world's least helpful list: "Something red. Something old. Something you can put things in. Something weird. . . ."

Well, you get the idea.

After completing the massive grocery shopping necessary for an extended family gathering the next day, I was just plain tired and cranky.

But no matter how hard it was to please my daughter, I could not let her down. Then her older sister came up with the solution. The local antique emporium was sure to have something that fit the list of criteria.

Owned by an extremely nice couple, the place was a dusty maze packed with treasures and, well, not-so-valuable items.

And it was absolutely the last place I wanted to go.

Three years previously, I had left the place in tears after selling them my grandmother's silver flatware and my treasured composition ballerina doll. That year had been difficult, and though I told myself that things are only things, it hurt to trade my remaining cherished possessions for mundane items such as electricity and food. The shame of crying in public over it only made matters worse.

Still, after this period of time and with a grossly swollen face as a disguise, it was unlikely the owners would recognize me.

And, sure enough, the place offered gifts for every possible taste.

A one-eyed, stuffed baby alligator certainly qualified as "weird" in my book, while the antique red lacquered box earned points in at least two of the desired categories.

We took our treasures to the counter. As one owner tallied and wrapped, the other studied my face. "Dental surgery," I muttered, wondering where his usually impeccable manners had gone.

He disappeared into the back room while I paid. But as we turned to leave, he reappeared with my old doll cradled in his arms. "We knew you didn't want to lose her. I figured eventually you'd come back," he said.

Maybe it was the painkillers because I didn't understand him at first. He held out the doll. "It's our Christmas present to you." Needless to say, there were hugs and tears all around, more than enough to embarrass my daughter.

The rest of the holiday went by in a blur. Dinner was prepared, gifts opened and most forgotten. I stopped looking like a chipmunk. The holiday season was officially over.

But that doll remains in my room, a reminder of the great and quiet kindness that lives around us every day of the year.

Lizanne Southgate

"Well I think wearing your daughter's homemade
Christmas tie is sweet."

Connecting at Christmas

*Blessed is the season which engages the
whole world in a conspiracy of love.*

Hamilton Wright Mabie

On a frosty December morning, I talked with my girls,
Lynsey and Laura, about God's gift to us in Jesus. I
reminded them how God gave us an undeserved gift, the
hope offered to us through the birth of Christ. The pure
love of our Heavenly Father who gave, without condition,
continued to amaze me.

"Then," I challenged, "how could we not respond to him
who loves us so?" I suggested doing a special family project to underscore the message of Christmas. Even though
they were children, I urged them to think about selfless
giving with no expectation to receive. "God uses servants
of all ages," I said.

Lynsey, then fifteen, popped up with, "We can make a
gift basket for one of the old people at church!" Living
with a teen had taught me to seize and rally around any
act of outward thoughtfulness, so I encouraged her idea.

Nine-year-old Laura chimed in, "Yeah, we can put stuff

together and give it to 'em for Christmas." We all agreed that a surprise gift basket would be our family project.

"Now, who'll be our recipient?" I asked. Laura suggested several names of senior citizens at church. After much discussion, we settled on "Mr. Paul."

Paul, known in our home as "Mr. Paul," was a cheerful, kind, rotund gent. He and his wife had a long, loving marriage, but no children. In fact, except for his wife, Mr. Paul had no living family. Each Sunday, Mr. Paul and his wife faithfully worked in the church's sound booth recording services for the homebound. They felt it was their ministry. They also felt it was their ministry to "hush" the children chattering in the hall. Often, they were the eyes and ears of absent parents.

But early that year, Mr. Paul's wife had received a diagnosis of terminal cancer. Within months, his world changed as he buried his wife and partner of fifty years. We knew it'd be a particularly lonely Christmas for Mr. Paul.

Parties, shopping, rehearsals, baking, and festive dinners filled our weeks following that family project discussion. We were busy, yet through the demanding schedule, we each thought of Mr. Paul.

Lynsey found an attractive basket large enough to hold a multitude of tiny treasures, including lip balm, aftershave, and a package of chocolate truffles. While baking, we set aside homemade cookies and candy for Mr. Paul. On shopping trips, Laura always found an unusual keepsake and, eyes twinkling, would say, "Mr. Paul will like this!" Then we'd tuck her chosen gift in our shopping cart. Lynsey made a Christmas card, and Dad jumped in with gift suggestions from a man's point of view: a tie, devotional book, and wallet. Together, we came up with a variety of presents to pack in our gift basket. We imagined Mr. Paul's reaction.

Lynsey thought he'd cry.

Laura said he'd laugh.

The time spent focusing on another person gave me multiple opportunities to remind my girls of God's gift to us—how satisfied God was in giving of his treasure. As our basket and anticipation swelled, my girls began arguing over which one would offer it. We hurriedly put in our final treats, and Laura cheerfully decorated the basket. Her homemade bow and carefully placed tissue paper made it a beautiful gift.

The Sunday before Christmas arrived, and our family eagerly but gently carried the bulging basket into church. Lynsey and Laura both held onto the handle, each afraid the other would get all the credit. My husband and I followed close behind.

Mr. Paul sat in his small, glass-enclosed cubicle turning knobs on a complex control panel. The girls stumbled over each other in their eagerness to get up the two steps to his level. Hearing the commotion, he turned toward them. When his eyes fell on the basket, my girls shouted, "Merry Christmas!" and shoved it in his direction. With a look of genuine surprise, he reached out to accept our gift. His aged arms cradled it as tears welled up in his blue eyes. For a moment, there was silence, but he spoke volumes through his grateful expression.

My girls still muse over that year of our first family project when the Christmas message lived in their hearts—a gift given, a gift received.

Brenda Nixon

The Focus

Last Christmas I decided to let Stephen, my four-year-old grandson, help me decorate for Christmas. We keep two sets of nativity figures, one of ivory porcelain and the other of teakwood. I took the porcelain set to the hutch in the dining area, then assigned Stephen to assemble the wooden set on a low table in the living room.

I helped him remove the newspaper wrappings on the figurines of Mary, Joseph, baby Jesus, the manger, an angel, two shepherds, two sheep, three wise men, and three camels. Then I left him to arrange them as he wanted.

In the dining room, I opened the glass door of the hutch and carefully placed the beautiful porcelain Mary, Joseph, and the baby in the center of the top shelf. I symmetrically spread shepherds and sheep on one side, and wise men and camels on the other. Then I surrounded the scene with green garlands tied with red velvet bows. When I turned on the light in the hutch, it illuminated the glorious scene. Satisfied, I closed the door and set about unpacking snowmen and other novelties of the season. When I happened to glance in the living room to see how Stephen was doing, his arrangement stopped me in my tracks.

Stephen had placed baby Jesus and the manger in the center as I had, but he had crowded the rest of the figures— even the camels—around the manger in a tight circle. The only figures he needed to place were the two small sheep. I wondered what he would do since there didn't seem to be any more room. Apparently, Stephen was also wondering as he stood there clapping the wooden sheep together. Then I think he must have remembered how he felt as a little boy trying to see a parade with so many adults in his way because he squeezed one sheep between a shepherd's legs and the other between a camel and Mary. Stephen stood back and admired his work. Now everyone could see what he came there to see!

Focus, I thought. *It's all in the focus.*

Pauline Youd

"... And he was born in a stable, 'cuz there was
no room for him in the church."

Dad's Christmas Gift

*This is Christmas: not the tinsel,
not the giving and receiving, not even
the carols, but the humble heart that receives
a new wondrous gift, the Christ.*

Frank McGibben

It is that time of year again, and I find myself caught up in the hustle and bustle of the holiday season just like the rest of the busy, last-minute shoppers. Christmas carols are softly playing over the loudspeakers in all the stores, but they can scarcely be heard over the other noises. "Have a good Christmas!" "No, honey, you can't have that, and besides Santa will soon be here!" And who could forget the all-too-familiar lament, "I'm so tired of this. I can't find anything. Everything is picked over."

I'm not at the mall, though, to buy last-minute gifts. I'm here to make a "deposit." I sit for a moment and watch as the busy shoppers, families, frantic husbands, young lovers, and the occasional teenager all rush about, loaded down with bags. Some of them display bright, smiling faces, while others are wiping the sweat from their brows, cursing the fact that they decided to wear their winter coat, even though there is no snow on the ground.

I gaze around and wonder if this creation was meant to be. Certainly, this was not part of the master plan two thousand years ago when God sent the newborn baby Jesus to redeem and save us.

How is it that we allowed ourselves to get so caught up in the commercial aspect of this joyous holiday season? Oh, sure, the mall does its part by putting out the very beautiful nativity scene with the brightly colored garments, the realistic animals, the cute baby Jesus—and who could forget those interesting wise men!

I turn my head toward this year's nativity display and watch the little children pointing at the donkey, oohing and ahhing over the manger. It is obvious they appreciate the true meaning of Christmas at this exact moment. Many of them will take part in Christmas pageants in their own churches, while other families, unfortunately, cannot provide a Christmas with gifts and a large feast for their children. *A sad reality,* I find myself thinking out loud, and then I say a silent prayer for those innocent kids who may never have anyone teach them the true meaning of the holiday season.

I look around and see that the merchants are all smiling and full of glee. Sales are down this year—people have moved to other parts of the country—but things are going great today. Yes, they are on par with last year's sales for Christmas Eve. Again, I muse, surely this could never be God's plan.

I turn my attention to the other end of the mall and see one of my coworkers. She looks tired and frazzled. *No wonder,* I think to myself, *she has been preparing for the holidays since early November.* My coworker put up her tree weeks ago, and now dust is settling on the stairway garland that she painstakingly put in place with the tenacity of Martha

Stewart. I let my mind wander back for a few moments, and I recall a conversation I had with my daughter as we left this woman's house three weeks earlier. As we walked back to our car, Emily looked up at me and said, "Mommy, how come we don't have our tree up yet? Won't Christmas soon be here?"

"Yes, honey, it will—in three more weeks." Then I thought of the best reason to explain why our house still looked bare.

"Darling," I said, "your birthday is next month. I think when we take down the tree, I'll put up balloons and streamers and decorate the whole house for your party."

"Don't be silly, Mommy. My birthday isn't for a long time after Christmas. It would be foolish to decorate so early!"

"Oh, really? Do you know why we have Christmas?"

"Gee, Mommy, you really are being silly. Of course I know why we have Christmas. It's Jesus's birthday."

"Exactly, my dear," I replied. "And if you think it is silly to start decorating for your birthday three weeks early, don't you think it is equally foolish to start decorating for Jesus's birthday too soon?"

She nodded her head in agreement and gave my hand a little squeeze. It was our silent understanding that we both knew and understood the true meaning of Christmas.

My thoughts quickly came back to the present as my coworker approached me. "Taking a little break, are you? Have you got all your shopping done?" she asked.

"As much as I am going to do," I told her. "I'm not here to shop. I just have a deposit to make."

"Oh, well," she said, "I have no money left to put in the bank. In fact, I just had to take more out to pay for these few gifts I had forgotten about." She laid down several large packages that weighed heavily in her arms.

"I wish my crowd would give up this gift-giving thing. You can't buy anything for ten dollars now. And what do you get for a teenage boy anyway? My nerves are gone. I can't wait to get back to work to get my check—God knows I'm gonna need it."

I sat in silence as she bent to retrieve her parcels, but as she turned to leave, I said, "Maybe we can get together over the holidays. Give me a call, and I'll prepare a nice meal for us all."

"That would be perfect," she shouted as she waved her one free hand and made her way into the nearby sporting goods store.

I glanced at my watch and gathered up my gloves, my purse, and my thoughts. I decided that the time had arrived. I would put it off no longer. My eyes started to fill with tears as I made my way through the center of the mall. I was here to carry on a tradition that my poor father had started so many years ago. Each time I thought of him, my heart ached a little more, especially at Christmastime. This year would mark the fourteenth anniversary of his death. He had been a loving and generous man who always found time to help others. Financially, he was probably the poorest man in our hometown, but we had the richest family—in love, in giving, in caring, and in understanding the needs of those who were less fortunate than ourselves.

I reached the "kettle" and was greeted by the smiling faces of two Salvation Army officers.

"God bless you, my love, and Merry Christmas!" said the man in the neatly pressed uniform. His eyes were like twinkling stars, and he was grinning from ear to ear.

"God bless you, too, and Merry Christmas to you and yours as well," I replied as I deposited a twenty-dollar bill into the plastic ball. I was doing this now, not only in memory of my father, who always made the annual trip to the Salvation Army kettle, but also for my own son and daughter. Hopefully, they would carry on the tradition when I passed on, knowing that they, too, had been taught the true meaning of Christmas as my dad had taught me— the gift of knowing that it is indeed better to give than to receive.

I joined the throng of the other shoppers and made my way back home. My family would be waiting for me. I envisioned the scene that would greet me. My husband would be standing over a piping hot pot of soup (all ready for the friends and family who would show up tonight after the late evening church service). My son, Luke, would be busy belting out the newest Christmas carol he had learned to play on one of the many musical instruments he owned. (God had truly blessed him with the gift of music.) Emily would be waiting at the top of the stairs with the baby Jesus in her hand. She would greet *me* with an emphatic, "Mommy, it's time now to put the baby in the nativity scene. What took you so long?" I'd scoop her up and say, "Yes, it is time, sweetheart." Then I'd move into the living room, freshly decorated with trinkets and treasures from past Christmases together, and as I would watch my daughter carefully lay the Christ child in the manger, I'd bow my head and say, "Merry Christmas, Dad, and Happy Birthday, Jesus."

Kimberly Welsh

The Gift of Time

*What wisdom can you find that
is greater than kindness?*

Jean Jacques Rousseau

I was a Christmas baby, and today was my tenth birthday, making it extra special. After opening our presents and eating Christmas brunch with Mum and Dad, my big sister Gail and I scooted upstairs to our bedroom to try out some of our gifts. She was placing a stack of 45-rpm records on the spindle of the record player, and I was about to model another of my new sweaters when Mum called up to us.

"Carol! Gail! Are you two dressed yet? We're leaving soon to visit your grandmother. Hurry up! She'll be expecting us!"

Gail and I exchanged pained looks. Don't get me wrong: we dearly loved our Gramma White, but visiting a nursing home on Christmas Day was not our idea of fun. We shrugged our shoulders in joint resignation and started to get dressed.

Gramma White had been living with us for the past three years, but a month ago she fell and broke her hip.

During her hospital stay, Dad and Mum held a family conference and explained that Gramma could not return home. She needed greater care than we could provide. When she was released from the hospital, she was transferred to a nearby nursing home. Mum visited her almost every day. Gail and I dropped in to say hello a few times on our way home from school. The white metal beds and side tables were all the same, and everything else was painted in varying shades of pale green. Gramma usually remembered who we were, but sometimes she didn't, and we would coax her into conversation by talking about the old days at the cottage. The dry air was always too warm and tainted with the odors of illness and aging. I felt uncomfortable standing next to her bed in a large room filled with other old people. Our visits were usually very short.

Christmas was Gramma's favorite time of year. As the holiday season approached, the decorations hung by the staff made her aware that this would be her first Christmas away from home and family. She felt very sad. So to cheer up Gramma we told her we would bring Christmas to her. It was time to keep our promise.

Gail and I came downstairs to the kitchen where Mum approved of our outfits and put the finishing touches on our hair. It was just a five-minute drive to the home.

We entered the lobby area where the communal Christmas tree was lighted, but the hallways were empty, and our footsteps echoed hollowly in the stairwell as we walked to the second floor. When we passed the long line of beds in the ward, I noticed most of the patients were sleeping and that we seemed to be the only visitors. When Gramma saw us, she smiled and responded happily to our hugs and Merry Christmas wishes. She was enjoying the day! We had a wonderful time while opening gifts, telling tales of Christmas past, and even singing carols.

Dad also noticed that few of the other patients had visitors. He remained quiet and seemed deep in thought while we continued to chat with Gramma. Then he excused himself and left the ward.

He returned carrying some cartons of ice cream and paper cups from the cafeteria. He explained his plan: Christmas was a time for family to celebrate the joy of the season together with loved ones. If, for whatever reason, family and friends couldn't be there for some of the other patients, then we would substitute and bring the spirit of Christmas to them. While Mum stayed with Gramma, the three of us went visiting. Dad took Gail and me across the hall and explained our mission to the nurse, who was more than happy to assist. He went back to visit with Gramma while the nurse took Gail and me around the ward.

As a shy ten-year-old, I was very nervous at first. I didn't know any of these people, and they didn't know me. Sadly, some of them were a little confused and even uncertain about what was so special about this particular day. The nurse escorted me to the bedside of my first challenge and pointed out the patient's name taped at the foot of her bed. After a moment's hesitation, I summoned the courage to introduce myself and offer her some ice cream. Although the memory of her name has faded over the years, I still recall our conversation. She declined the treat, but smiled and told me she had a granddaughter about my age who lived out West. She asked me to sit and tell her what I got for Christmas, and when she found out it was my birthday, too, she hugged me!

That first successful stop helped me overcome my stage fright, and as I moved from bed to bed, the heartwarming smiles and kind comments from each resident gave me confidence. I really began to get into the spirit of things. I especially remember my last stop.

I had just two cups of ice cream left, and I was saving one for myself. The occupant of that final bed was a very frail-looking woman. A halo of soft white hair framed her heavily lined face, and her head was sunk deeply into the pillow. She appeared to be asleep. I sat in the chair beside her bed and said softly, "Merry Christmas. Would you like some ice cream?"

Her eyelids fluttered and then opened wide, revealing a pair of bright blue eyes. She frowned, then fixed her gaze on me and spoke hesitatingly, "But I don't have any money."

"That's okay," I replied. "They're free."

"Oh," she said, as a bright smile spread across her face, erasing decades of age, "then I'll have two."

I opened both of the ice-cream cups, unwrapped a wooden spoon, and passed them to her.

We talked while she ate.

That was almost fifty Christmases ago, but I can still picture those sparkling blue eyes and recall the wonderful feeling that came from giving another the priceless gift of my time.

Carol (Pearce) Forrest as told to John Forrest

The Nativity Story

We stumbled upon the manger scene one December night. It was a live nativity scene in front of a small church. I was on the way home from a Christmas party with my two children, nine and six, who had jumped and played and eaten too much pizza, cake, and candy canes. The excitement of the season had reached an almost unbearable climax as they discussed what Santa might bring this year.

While driving, I pointed out, "Oh, look a live nativity scene!" My six-year-old exclaimed, "A donkey! Let's go see." The traffic was heavy with Christmas shoppers, and it would take a few maneuvers and more patience than I had after two hours in a Jumping Party Zone with thirty-plus children giddy on holiday snacks, but I nevertheless decided to add this wonderful, unanticipated reminder of the season to our agenda. I made a U-turn and waited for traffic to clear.

Only a few cars were there when we finally turned into the parking lot of the small church. I guess many others' mental flipping of the coin had landed the other way, and they had decided to keep driving and stick to the to-do list they had so close to Christmas.

We walked toward the scene. It was sweet and not elaborate, what one would expect of a small church production. There were no words, other than those from the audience milling about, sipping hot cocoa, and talking quietly. We were welcomed by a woman with smiling eyes, and I commented, "We were just driving by and had to stop."

"That's the point," the woman said kindly. "We're glad you did. The kids can feed the donkey and the goats if they'd like."

If they'd like? I thought. *Are you kidding me?* The feeding of livestock was the point of our stopping. They were not able to see baby Jesus from the busy street, after all.

The kids moseyed toward the goats first and petted them, but the donkey was the main attraction. They measured food into their hands and offered it to the animal. The donkey did not seem very interested, but he did try to take a nibble at my son's elbow. Both of the kids giggled.

After the donkey incident, I watched my daughter, Shelby, as she walked toward the manger scene. It had taken a while for her to turn her full attention to it as the distractions of the animals had kept her busy. But now I could see in her face the slow recognition of the scene in front of her. She walked sideways, tentatively and slowly gazing at the little stable scene, lit by a bright spotlight. The cast included Mary, Joseph, and several toddlers dressed as angels, complete with golden garland looping their small heads.

I witnessed a most striking image that burned into my memory forever—my nine-year-old daughter walking in front of that spotlight. With clarity on her face, she realized that she had wandered into the light that was meant for Jesus. She humbly walked to the side, joining the audience of witnesses.

I was tearful nearly the whole way home. In-between admonishing the kids not to touch each other with their livestock-contaminated hands, I played the moment with Shelby's viewing over and over in my mind.

The moments we had just shared were a perfect metaphor for the season. The busy traffic and parties had nearly kept us away from the story of Jesus. I had come inches from not stopping, from not taking the time and energy.

I thought of my children kneeling at the side of that pen, their intensity focused on ensuring that the goats were full and happy. And I remembered, most of all, the light cast on the baby Jesus, illuminating him and my children's images.

This Christmas I pray for a child's humble eyes to see the meaning I witnessed. I pray that, not just at Christmas, but during all the days of this life, I am able to follow the light of what's truly important, to follow the to-do list placed before me by the Holy Spirit and not placed on me by the distractions of this world. As I drove home that dark evening, I recounted what I had said when we stopped. "We were just driving by and had to stop." And then the prophetic words spoken straight from God, I now believe, "That's the point." To notice the light and stop.

Amy Breitmann

Reprinted with permission of Jonny Hawkins. ©2007 Jonny Hawkins.

2

THROUGH THE EYES OF A CHILD

If you can't accept anything on faith, you are doomed to a life dominated by doubt.

Kris Kringle, Miracle on 34th Street

Once a Year

The only gift is a portion of thyself.

Ralph Waldo Emerson

"Lindy," the young boy whispered. His eager tug continued at her sleeve until his little sister's curly head turned on her pillow.

"Lindy, wake up. It's Christmas." The words were like cold water to the six-year-old's eyes, wakening her from a deep sleep. Sitting up, she blinked and peered around. It was still dark, but it was an unspoken rule that once you woke up after falling asleep, no matter the time, it was officially Christmas morning. So she pushed her blankets aside and let her other older brother take her by the hand and lead her to the staircase.

Although Lindy was the youngest of five children, this time with her brothers and sister was a secret delight of her own. For it was on this special day of the year that she was willingly included in their adventure. She smiled inwardly, her heart picking up its pace as anticipation set in. Each child would gasp when his or her name was on a particularly large present. With eager fingers, they would

tear the many tiny packages their mother had painstakingly wrapped to fill their stockings.

The two middle boys giggled as they took turns sliding
down the long, wooden banister.

"Shh," the oldest sister warned with a wide smile.
"You're going to wake up Mom and Dad." She turned to
Lindy, taking her other hand. "Come on, Lin."

The warm fuzzies in Lindy's stomach grew to near
exploding. Willingly, she let her sister and brother take
her down the orange carpeted stairs. *If they only knew,* she
thought to herself, but she knew she would never tell
them. Taken by the hand, escorted into their plans with
excitement and such gentle care, was Lindy's best
Christmas gift ever.

Lindy B. Dolan

Christmas in the Heart of a Child

Every child comes with a message that
God is not yet discouraged of man.

Rabindranth Tagore

It was my turn at church to serve communion to the elderly people who can't make it to the church services. Kallie went with me, clinging to her Beanie Baby. She loved that doll more than anything!

We went to serve the first person on our list at a local nursing home. He was a kindly old gentleman named George. I had visited him before. He was pleasant and physically spry for his age. He seemed happy to see us. My daughter communicates well with the elderly. She immediately gave him a big hug (Beanie Baby and all). The smile on his face seemed to grow from the depths of his heart. There is nothing like the love of a little child to brighten one's day.

I asked George if he had any family around, and he said no. I asked him how he had been doing, to which he replied, "Not very well." He said he just wasn't having a good day. However, George maintained a great attitude about his health, and he knew that God was in control. As

I glanced over at my daughter, I could see the sympathy in her eyes. It was the kind that only a child can feel in her somewhat limited understanding of an adult world, but a pure kind of sympathy that knows no age boundaries.

After I had served communion, we started saying our good-byes, but as he did the last time I visited him, George got up and said he would walk us out. He said it was good for him to get up and walk from time to time. When we exited the building, he kept on walking through the courtyard with us, right to the gate out by the street. I shook his hand and thanked him for walking us out. He seemed grateful to have had visitors and thanked us.

Then it happened—my daughter really caught me off guard. As she went to hug George good-bye, she held up her Beanie Baby and said, "You can have him." I found myself wanting to leap forward and say, "No, you don't have to . . ." but I was frozen in my tracks. George bent down and took it from her with a smile and a hug. I was stunned. My mind was trying to comprehend what I had just witnessed. My eight-year-old daughter had just shown me Christ in action. Her love and compassion were a natural and immediate manifestation of her love and obedience. What self-sacrifice! I could only hope and pray to love and give so willingly.

As we made our way to my truck, I turned and looked back at George. Burned into my mind forever would be the memory of a bent-over old man, who had just been touched by God through the heart of a little child, shuffling back to his confinement and clutching a little smiley-faced Beanie Baby.

My vision was blurred from watery eyes as I told my daughter how much I loved her and how proud I was of her. "You just made God smile!"

Lane Clayton as told to Joan Clayton

A Little Angel's Big Prayer

*While we try to teach our children all about
life, our children teach us what life is all about.*

Unknown

When I heard my father's voice on our answering machine that day six years ago, I knew instantly why he was calling. He is far too deaf to use a phone anymore. It had to mean that my mother had died.

And she had, quite suddenly. The demands of organizing the funeral pushed us through the next days, held up by a chain of prayer with links all over the world. Her recent illness meant that, despite the pain of our loss, this really was her Lord's reprieve. My sister and I both felt this, which made my mother feel very close to us.

But my father seemed encased in a mountain of ice, moving through the hours in sad-faced silence. Her near-constant companion for sixty years, he couldn't visualize life without her—and didn't seem to want to try.

I was relieved when he accepted my offer to stay on with him for a week after every one else had left. But, eventually, I had to return home, too. He lasted six days on his own, then collapsed. My sister brought him back to her new home, midway between his Florida one and mine in New Hampshire. He was admitted to a nearby hospital for surgery, and for the second time in three weeks, I boarded a plane on short notice.

I was appalled when I saw him. My sister and I knew that, regardless of his illness, he was really fighting to find the will to live—and might not succeed. My prayers begged God to sustain him, to help him feel God's love, as well as ours. But as Dad became increasingly unresponsive, my heart sank more heavily than ever.

On Christmas Eve, I asked God to help me do what I could, surrender to him what I couldn't, and trust that he held Dad in his loving hands, whatever the outcome.

I forced myself to go to the hospital the next morning, where I was astonished to see Dad sitting up. Though he'd been immobile in bed for nearly two weeks, he had taken not one, but two walks that morning, the nurse told me.

His eyes were very bright when I arrived. "Hon, I've got to get out of here," he said. "Your mother sent a little angel last night, who told me that's what God wants me to do— get up and go on with my life."

As if to test his sincerity, circumstances prevented his discharge on the holiday, which meant I had a chance to learn more about that "little angel" when a friend called to wish me a happy Christmas.

A treasured prayer companion, she has an admirable godmother's relationship with her five-year-old nephew. She takes her duty to champion his spiritual life very seriously, and they talk together about God all the time.

"Tristan was here Sunday," she said. "We found a scraggly branch, stuck it in the snow, and made a Charlie Brown Christmas tree. As we decorated it, he looked at me and asked, 'Auntie Di, are you okay?'"

"I told him I've been worried about my friend because her mommy died, and her daddy's been so sad that nobody knows what to do."

She described how the little boy paused for a moment, then said, "Well, of *course* the daddy's sad. The *mommy* died!"

His clear, child's wisdom brought sudden tears for me as I listened.

Then she shared his next words. "But God can make anything better, right Auntie Di? Tomorrow's special because it's Jesus's birthday. I'm going to ask God to tell the Daddy that the Mummy is with Jesus, and that everything is going to be okay."

There was a long, teary silence on my end as she finished.

On Christmas Eve, that little boy had offered his faith-filled, confident prayer, and that Christmas, through the power of such prayer, was a turning point for my dad. He will remember it always as the season when, warmed by the light of the world and touched by a little angel, he found the will to live.

Phyllis Ring

Sarah's Christmas Wish

Sarah, my three-year-old daughter, wanted to see Santa before Christmas as this would be her first time to sit on his lap and tell him what she wanted. When my wife and I practiced with her, we would ask what she wanted Santa to bring, and she always responded, "I want a bear and presents."

So Sarah, her mom, and Grammy went to see Santa at the local mall. Sarah was ready. She confidently walked up to Santa when it was her turn. Mom and Grammy stayed back to take in the whole experience.

She jumped up on Santa's lap, and when he asked what she wanted for Christmas, she looked at him and gave her response. As soon as the words came out, Santa began to laugh uncontrollably. Sarah was bouncing up and down on his lap. Santa quickly regained his composure and again asked her what she wanted. She again told him her wish—and again he started to laugh!

Getting a little nervous, Mom walked up to Santa and asked him what she had said.

"I have never had a child ask for this before," Santa replied between his chuckles. "When I asked her what she wanted me to bring her, she told me she wanted a beer!"

William Livers

The Wish List

With just a few weeks left before Christmas, I was overwhelmed with keeping up with my full-time job, housework, and all the preparations for the holidays. My five-year-old daughter, Nikki, was always right under my feet, trying to act older. She always wanted to "help" with everything.

On this particular day, she was more of a hindrance than a help. "Why don't you go write Santa a list of what you want for Christmas," I suggested.

"But I want to help you," she replied.

Not being in the mood for a little "adult" following me, I answered, "Do as I say, Nikki. Go write a Christmas list for Santa."

"Okay," she mumbled and ran up the stairs to complete her assignment.

As I finished up the housework, I began to imagine the expensive items that would appear on her list. There would probably be a video system, a doll house, and maybe a new bike. Boy, I set myself up for that one!

Later that night, I saw Nikki's list on the table. There were only two words on it. "Nikki," I yelled up the stairs, "come down here!"

She flew down the stairs in her pajamas and looked up at me. I showed her the list and said, "Why do you have these two things on your list? You already have a dog and a cat."

"I know," my little five-year-old said to me, "but they're the only words I know how to spell."

Cheryl M. Kremer

Reprinted by permission of Off the Mark and Mark Parisi. ©2007 Mark Parisi.

Love for Tots

*Christmas, my child, is love in action.
Every time we love, we give. It's Christmas.*

Dale Evans Rogers

On a late November day, my family went to see the play, *A Christmas Carol.* We were just loading into the car when I blurted out, "I feel bad for all those poor children who don't have what we have for Christmas." I was surprised by my own words. Why had that picture of little, sick Tiny Tim popped into my head?

"You are right, Lynnea. Many people don't have all the holiday presents and merriment that you have." My papa obviously agreed with my statement. I thought all about what had just happened the whole ride. When my mama and papa told me they were cutting down on the presents, why did I feel bad for myself when others didn't get anything?

After I'd thought about the situation for about a week, I was very happy for the weekend to come. I sped down the stairs into the basement. I dug around in an old hamper and pulled out a scruffy brown teddy bear with a plaid bow around its neck. I smiled wide, admiring the toy. *If I can make a difference this Christmas, this is it!* I thought, holding the fluffy teddy bear in my arms. I skipped upstairs and explained my planned good deed to my mom. I saw a twinkle in her eyes.

The next week, my mom took me to the local mall. I rode the escalator with glee and excitement. I couldn't wait! When we arrived at a small table draped in a white cloth, a man dressed in a military uniform greeted us. He was a bit stiff, but kind. He pointed to a golden box labeled "Toys for Tots" in big red letters. I placed my teddy bear in the small pile of toys. I knew I was doing something right, and my heart was filled with warmth. I smiled at the man, grasped my mom's hand, and walked away. I thought about a child suffering from poverty. Her eyes would glitter as she looked at the teddy bear—the glittering eyes of sheer joy, happiness, and thankfulness.

Lynnea Bolin

Tree of Thanks

*Gifts of time and love are surely the
basic ingredients of Christmas.*

Peg Bracker

"How can we honor your teachers this year?" I asked
my two young daughters one cold December morning. As
a way to teach them to show appreciation, I always
involved my kids in making and giving a Christmas gift to
their teachers.

"Let's bake some cookies," my older daughter, Lynsey,
piped up.

"Yeah, we can decorate them in pretty colors," chimed in
little Laura.

"That's a nice idea, girls," I replied. "What about something different? Maybe something very unusual."

"I like my teacher," Laura declared with a big grin
revealing her lost front tooth.

"Good," I affirmed with a pat on her back.

"Can we make my teacher a handkerchief?" Lynsey
asked.

"Well, that'd be special," I said, "but I don't know how to

sew or embroider. I'm a better cook than a seamstress."

"What can we bake, Mom?" Laura asked.

"Hmm, what do you like to eat?" I asked.

"Those crunchy, sticky bars!" they yelled together.

"Oh, when I mix the marshmallows and rice cereal?"

"Yeah, they're so good!"

Instead of making the standard bars, I suddenly thought, we could shape the mixture into a cone so it looks like a tree. Then, we could decorate with gumdrops, string licorice, and red and green sugar. "Hey, girls, what if you help me melt the butter and marshmallows?"

"Yeah! That'd be neat, Mom," Lynsey agreed. She and her sister began dancing around the room like drops of water in a hot skillet.

Through the clang of metal cookwear, we dragged out a round, deep pan. Then Lynsey retrieved the butter, marshmallows, and vanilla, while Laura found the green food coloring, multicolored sprinkles, and cereal. Instead of the traditional rice cereal, I wanted to use something round like Cap'n Crunch or Cheerios.

Lynsey, Laura, and I melted the butter and gooey marshmallows. Each took turns stirring, watching it gradually come to a soft boil. I mixed in green coloring and Cheerios, then we buttered our hands to shape the warm combination into a cone. The warmth in the kitchen and on our hands was soothing, and I easily forgot the chaos in my kitchen. "Let's press these into the tree to look like garland," I said, handing them red licorice strings. I could see a tremendous surge of self-esteem and new energy in my kids. We laughed together as we made a sweet treat for each teacher.

"I want to shake on colored sugar," Laura insisted, squeezing my arm with anticipation. "I can't wait to give mine to Mrs. Smith." Then she turned and gave me an impulsive hug, leaving buttery prints on my sleeve.

Our bejeweled cone looked just like an ornate Christmas tree!

Early Monday morning, we carefully placed each finished product on wax paper, then transferred it onto a sturdy foam plate. I drove to the school where Lynsey and Laura climbed out of the car with their treasures in hand. They skipped up to the front of the building and waited for me to park and join them.

Inside, teachers and children passed us in the hallway, hungrily eyeing our detailed project. "Wow, that looks yummy," one teacher remarked.

"Yeah, we're giving this to Mrs. Smith," Laura proudly announced.

"I've got one for my teacher, too," Lynsey added.

I accompanied Laura into her classroom to "ahhs" from the children. "Look," she yelled at her teacher. "Here's a gift for you because I like you."

"Oh my, Laura," the teacher responded, bending down to Laura's level and reaching out to take the plate. "What a nice surprise!"

"I made it myself, just for you!"

"Well, you can be proud."

"I am!"

"You know," said Laura's teacher, "cooking helps you understand more about math because you have to measure and know your fractions. Plus you get to spend special time with your mom and sister."

I thanked the teacher for her faithful commitment to my daughter and left the room to join Lynsey, who was anxiously pacing in the hallway. She and I walked into her class with a déjà vu of admiration. Lynsey's tree looked like artwork. The edible glitter glistened like a frost-covered lawn. She had also cut out a paper star and carefully printed her teacher's name in the middle. Then she had taped the paper star to a toothpick and inserted it on top of the tree.

"Lynsey, you created a unique masterpiece," her teacher said.

"Thank you," Lynsey, replied looking a little self-conscious. Then she turned over her appreciation gift to the teacher.

Every year, we've tried to design unique and useful presents for the teachers who do so much for my kids throughout the year. Often, we work on a craft project, but cooking with my kids always wins hands down.

Brenda Nixon

3

THE SANTA FILES

. . . The stockings were hung by the chimney with care,

In hopes that St. Nicholas soon would be there. . . .

Clement C. Moore,
The Night Before Christmas

Memories of a Christmas Doll

*The children were nestled all
snug in their beds, while visions of sugar
plums danced in their heads. . . .*

Clement C. Moore,
The Night Before Christmas

The train rounded the bend a quarter-mile from the station with its headlight bright, even in the afternoon sunshine. I held onto my mother's hand as I pointed with my left, on tiptoes in excitement and anticipation, knowing my grandmother was arriving from Manhattan, Kansas, to spend Christmas with us in St. Louis. I missed school that afternoon to meet the train, my first-grade skills sufficient to allow the privilege of going to an outlying station near Forest Park to welcome her. Grandma came every December for several weeks until her death after Christmas in 1958. Each visit in the later years was memorable. We spent the evenings playing games, especially Rummy Royale around the kitchen table.

The Christmas I was six in 1954, however, holds a different memory, for it was the year I learned the *truth* about

Santa Claus. Before Grandma came, we had decorated the balsam fir Dad had placed in the corner of the living room, the large, colored bulbs of that era reflecting in the tinsel that dangled precariously on the branches. It was especially beautiful through young, squinting eyes that blurred the tree into a shimmering mass.

Mysterious boxes were appearing daily beneath the tree, and the countdown was on until the morning when all would be revealed. I had been asked what I wanted Santa to bring me that year, and a "bride doll" was always my quick response. I had great confidence that despite not having a fireplace and chimney, St. Nick would find a way to enter our home with the desired gift.

My older brother and I shared a room across the hall from our parents in the small, two-bedroom house on the corner of Big Bend Boulevard and Exeter in Shrewsbury, Missouri. Across the shaded side street began the lovely community of Webster Groves. We moved into a large, three-story house in Webster before I entered the second grade, outgrowing our Big Bend house when my younger brother, Peter, outgrew his crib. Many dear childhood memories remain of that suburban home where my parents and their oldest son and new daughter came to live after leaving Wichita, Kansas, three months after I was born. Christmas 1954 is one of those memories.

December 24 finally arrived that year, and our father continued the tradition of taking his children to downtown St. Louis to see the beautiful and enchanting department-store windows decorated for the holidays. Before malls started crawling across the landscape of suburbia, shoppers made their way to nearby cities to find the home furnishings and clothes needed for casual and formal living. This became one of the highlights of every year, an anticipated joy that allowed Mother the peace and quiet to finish baking and preparing for Christmas.

I saw many Santas that day: on street corners ringing bells for charity, near the toy sections in each department store we visited, outside the car window as we drove past even more displays. I was puzzled by all the Santas and determined that night I'd ask my older brother why there were so many. Since he knew everything anyway, he would undoubtedly have an answer.

Our beds on opposite walls, Kenny and I often talked at night before falling asleep, his extra six years of experience a helpful perspective on life. In the darkened room, lit only by the street lights outside our front-room window, I asked him about Santa Claus. He answered me with typical, twelve-year-old directness, "There's only one Santa that matters; the others are helpers dressed up to look like him. Our parents even help him."

Well, that made some sense. He challenged me to sneak downstairs to see what everyone was doing, perhaps to prove his point. And so I did.

The stairs ended at a landing, with several more steps into either the kitchen or the living room. I quietly made my way until I stopped at the last step before reaching the divide where I knew I'd be visible.

The kitchen light was on, a radio was softly playing Christmas carols, and my mother and grandmother were busy with a project that caught my attention. Absorbed as they were, they never saw me peek into the room. Mom was attentively ironing an ivory satin gown, a bridal gown to fit a doll, while Grandma was working on a veil. A lovely doll with blonde, gently curled hair that framed her porcelain face lay nearby on the table. My young heart knew at once this was to be the "bride doll" I requested.

Before creeping back upstairs, I glanced into the living room at the tree, bright with color, and festooned with an abundance of presents that had materialized since I'd kissed everyone good night and gone to bed.

I quickly got under the covers and told my brother what I'd seen. Apparently, our parents did help Santa provide the bounty of Christmas morning, but I decided to watch for his coming anyway, just to see what he'd bring. I dozed off and on in excitement, waking throughout the night to peer out the window at the stars, hoping to see Santa Claus streak across the sky. I never saw him, nor did I hear the sleigh bells jingle his arrival, but sleep overcame my desire to stay awake, and so I missed him.

We woke early on Christmas morning and eventually gathered together around the tree, under which more gifts had been added to indicate Santa had indeed come. When I first entered the living room, however, I only had eyes for the beautiful doll adorned in wedding finery, sitting serenely in a chair, a queen on a throne. She was the same one from the kitchen table, only transformed by her gown and veil.

I was told the doll had been given to my mother when she was a young girl in the years following her birth in 1910. Instructed to handle her carefully, I knew that meant I was to love her with gentle hands.

A doll was under the tree every Christmas after that, until in time I had acquired an enviable collection: a red-haired Ginny doll, a brunette Jill doll, Tiny Tears, and assorted dolls with wardrobes made by my mother.

December 1954 gave me an enlightened understanding of Santa Claus. The true generosity of the real St. Nicholas was aided by my grandmother, my parents, and the individuals who gave themselves to help children and others experience a blessed Christmas. His legendary spirit was alive and active in my parents throughout their lifetime, blessing our family with memories fine and dear. They made wonderful Santa's helpers!

Ann Greenleaf Wirtz

As previously appeared in the *Times News*, December 2006.

The Christmas Gift

A child's love is like a whisper,
given in little ways we do not hear. . . .
It is never ending
A blessing from above
Listen to the whispers of a child's love.

Sue Ellen Chandler

On Christmas Eve, I would be the only one in our home stirring, always the last to get to bed. I needed to stay up late to help Santa with his customary night's work.

Gifts that we could afford were wrapped and placed beneath an evergreen tree decorated for the most part with handmade ornaments. Our tree was tiny, but once decorated with our personal touch, it always seemed to have a peaceful, natural glow.

We had long tucked our little ones into their beds with their dreams of Christmas morning still dancing in their heads. (At least, I thought they were all fast asleep in their beds.) When I turned off the last of the living-room lights, I noticed one still on at the far end of the hall.

Quite surprised, I slipped silently down the hall toward the light, careful not to make a sound in hopes of seeing just what was going on in my wee lassie's room at this late-night hour. Her door was not quite shut, so I peeked in. I could see our sweet bonnie lass sitting alone on the floor of her room, struggling to wrap an old, tattered shoe box. She appeared to have all the right gear, only lacking the skill that would come in a few short years.

"Little one," I softly said, "what are you doing up so late and out of your bed? Santa may not come if you're still awake."

She replied, "Daddy, I wanted to give Santa a gift."

"But, sweetheart," I replied, "we left him shortbread and milk. He always likes that."

She sighed deeply as if to say that I just did not understand and then continued, "But, Daddy, this one is more special than that."

I sat down beside her and asked her to show me what made it so. One by one, she took from the box and laid before me all the special things never meant for me to see. One was a candy cane, half–eaten, that had once hung on our tree. She said, "This is so Santa will know the sweetness of Christmas shared with a friend."

Next was a child's game set of ball and jacks, one of her favorite games to play. My daughter explained, "This is so Santa knows the joy of playing and sharing my favorite toy." Then came a picture of the manger scene, one she had colored in Sunday school and went on to say, "This is a picture of baby Jesus with his mom and dad, so Santa can see the very first and best Christmas gift ever given to us all."

My heart began to melt. Raising my hand to my face, I wiped the tears that had welled up in my eyes.

Then, from the bottom of the box, she pulled out a red velvet hair ribbon, one she only wore for her Sunday best, and said, "And this is only so Santa knows that it's all from me. He will know because he first gave this ribbon to me."

A tear rolled down my cheek. Seeing and hearing of these gifts, so simple but dear, made it hard for me to speak, but I cleared the lump in my throat and spoke as best as I could. "Sweetheart, you are ever so right. These are much more special than cookies and milk. Let me help you finish your gift, and I'll put it under the tree right out front so Santa will be sure to see it first."

Smiling, she looked up at me and saw a tear still hanging on my cheek. She said, "Daddy, don't cry. Mommy and me already put your present under the tree."

We finished the wrapping and topped it with a golden bow. Satisfied the job had been done just right, she climbed into her bed, and I bid my little lassie a good night with a kiss on her sweet head.

I carried out her gift and knelt before the tree, placing it right out front as I had said I would, pausing for a moment to say a wee prayer of thanksgiving for the special gift of a child sent from above.

Santa did indeed receive the gift he had needed—and he will always treasure it—but even dearer to us is the gift of a child. For all the Christmases to come, and even when she is grown and out on her own, I know that in a special place is a gift of unselfish love and joy meant for Santa to open over and over again.

Raymond L. Morehead

Christmas at Six

At Christmas play, and make good cheer,
For Christmas comes but once a year.

Thomas Tusser

"All I want for Christmas is my two front teeth," played on the stereo three nights before Christmas while the fire crackled. My older sister was missing her two front teeth. Always a showoff, she danced around the room, acting out the song for the family. Everyone roared with laugher while the pine tree glowed and the tinsel shimmered. I was full of the Christmas spirit and hope that my Santa wish would come true.

Just after Thanksgiving, the Christmas catalogs appeared on the coffee table. Slowly turning the pages of the toy section, I selected all the things I wanted for Christmas in my mind. The list was growing when a picture of a log cabin filled the page—a real log cabin. I ran with the catalog to my mom and begged her to read the description: "Be the first to have your very own genuine log cabin made from real cedar logs."

I became obsessed with the log cabin, and thought about it day and night. It would be my own place. I'd put up curtains, have a slumber party with my friends, and be the happiest girl in the world. Around that time, my dad asked my brother and sisters if we had made out our wish lists. I was the youngest child and still needed help from my parents or sisters. My list was written in red and green crayon. Copying my sisters, it was bordered with blue stars, Christmas trees, and gingerbread men. Number one on the list, I wrote in red, with my best penmanship—"log cabin." That was it.

As the big day neared, my evening ritual was to recline on the carpet in the living room, stare up at the lights on the tree, and imagine how the log cabin would look sitting beside it with a big red bow. I would cut the red ribbon and enter the door to see an Easy Bake Oven in the corner.

Christmas Eve came, and my sisters and I sat on the couch as we did every year, and waited for Santa's sleigh and reindeer to come flying up the street and onto the roof. My eyes grew heavy as the neighborhood lights went out one by one. Dad told my sisters it was time to turn in as he picked me up and carried me to bed.

The rule for Christmas morning was that no one was allowed into the living room until the music played. Pacing in our room for an hour drove us crazy with excitement. In that time, I imagined the log cabin in every possible position in the living room. At last, "Joy to the World" sang out, and my sisters blasted out ahead of me. My brother came thundering down the hall, swooped me up, and flew me into the living room like an airplane—sound effects and all. "ZZOOOOMMMM!"

"MERRY CHRISTMAS!" I shouted.

While hugging Mom and Dad, I scanned the room for the log cabin. It was nowhere in sight.

"Here's something from Santa," yelled my sister.

She ripped off the shiny paper and screamed with delight.

"It was on my list!"

For the next forty-five minutes, my family opened presents with the same delight—except me. I did my best to fool everyone that I, too, was happy.

"Look, sweetheart," said Mom, "here's something from Grandma."

I ripped open the present and found new pajamas. "These are pretty," I said.

"Just what you needed," said Mom. I smiled and held them close—a real Academy Award performance.

"Go ahead and put them on." As I walked down the hall, I thought maybe the cabin would be in the bathroom—a glimmer of hope that quickly faded upon entering. In pretty pink floral pajamas, I continued pretending to love every gift I opened until I could take no more and burst into tears. Everyone stopped looking over their gifts and started laughing, which made me cry even more.

"Oh, what's this about?" asked Dad, picking me up. "I loved the clay coffee mug you made me." I sniffled and tried to say something.

"Wait a minute," said Dad. "I almost forgot there was a special delivery—something for you outside by the swing set."

"What!" I exclaimed, hugging him around the neck.

He put me down, and I ran out in the frosty air through the back yard and to the swing set where it sat—a genuine cedar log cabin.

It was even bigger in real life. I opened the door, entered, and gazed up at the ceiling. The smell of cedar filled the space. I stuck my head out the window and said, "It even smells good." I spent the rest of the morning playing inside and out of the cabin. My sisters teased me, while my brother complimented me on my acting skills. Mom and Dad sat on the swings, sipping their coffee and watching us all. I felt so special and was at that moment the happiest girl in the world. As for the Easy Bake Oven, I worked on that for the following year.

To this day, whenever my family gets together, we still have a good laugh about my "log cabin Christmas."

Kerry Germain

"I'll worry about the future later,
right now I'm really enjoying the present."

Here Comes Santa Claus

This year I had planned to start early—before Thanksgiving. I would take advantage of the extra time my special-needs son would need to "get acquainted" with Santa when there were no waiting lines. When my daughter was small, we would go to the mall to see Santa Claus. It was quite an ordeal. I would begin by selecting the perfect dress. Of course, accessories were carefully coordinated—socks, hair bows, shoes, etc. I would stand by as she sat with Santa, checking for a strand of hair across her face, a wrinkle in her dress, or some other detail that might make the picture less than perfect.

When my second child—a son—arrived, there was equal emphasis placed on his outfits, which had to be coordinated with my daughter in both color and style. Hats and caps became as important as hair bows and matching lace socks. Somehow, each time, I would leave the mall with picture in hand, knowing that despite the stress, I had captured the moment. How proud I was of these two little Christmas angels!

My third child, a little boy with autism, had an aversion to Santa pictures from the very beginning. My first Santa picture with the three of them was only a glimpse of

"Christmas Future." Though he was less than eight months old at the time, and significantly behind in physical developmental milestones, he had managed (despite Santa's best efforts to hold him) to avoid having his face in the picture. In the middle of a screaming rage, he had arched his back in such a way that his head was behind his body, and he was visible only from the waist down. I left the mall that day with a picture of Santa and two-and-a-half children.

Things only went downhill from there. For the next several years, attempts were made to photograph Santa and my youngest son, but to no avail. He would have no part of it. Each year, I dressed him in adorable outfits and continued to try. The child in me would not give up on capturing some of that magic of the season for him. We were on our way home from a neurotherapy appointment on a cold November day, and here I was again, in front of the mall, looking at that "window of opportunity." My older children were now too old for Santa pictures. I had a few minutes to spare. I looked at Paul in the backseat— evidence of lunch and snacks dominating what had started the day as a nice outfit. No matter, he always had spare clothes in his backpack.

In the parking lot, in the biting wind, we stripped off the soiled shirt. When I reached into the backpack for the spare, I pulled out an orange T-shirt—not exactly Christmas picture attire. I quickly dismissed this as a problem. Orange is a nice bright color and, hey, the shirt was clean. As I slid the shirt over my son's head, between the wind and the excitement of getting dressed in the parking lot, he had decided to be ticklish. He laughed, thrashed about, and resisted my every attempt to put on the shirt, stretching the neck of the shirt significantly before it was finally in place. Determined not to give up on the opportunity, we headed in to find Santa. Paul was excited about seeing Santa, actually requesting it, and I was not going to break the momentum. He resisted sitting on Santa's lap, but Santa and his helpers were patient. A small line began to form behind us as he circled around Santa, maintaining at least a three-foot distance. "We have to go," I said to him sadly. We had used up our time, and others were waiting.

"Take all the time you need," said Santa's helper. When Santa offered to read him a story, my son could no longer resist, and he settled into the chair beside Santa. He looked up in his orange T-shirt with the stretched-out neck, glasses crooked on his nose, and smiled broadly as the picture was snapped. "Would this picture be okay?" the assistant inquired as she let me take a look.

"Yes, it is *perfect*," I beamed.

What a lesson I have learned in this journey from perfection to reality. Yes, my life is more difficult and complicated having a special-needs child. Yes, there are times I am self-conscious, frustrated, and overwhelmed. But as I proudly carried my hard-earned Santa picture to the car, hand in hand with my little one, I realized that perfection is in the eyes of the beholder. And I have learned that through the eyes of a mother, all three of my children are absolutely perfect!

Carol Sue Hahn

Dear Santa

Santa, can you bring me a long forgotten smile?
Santa, can you bring me the happiness of a child?
Santa, can you just hold my hand
    and walk with me awhile?

Down memory lane we'll wander,
    while Christmas dreams do rush,
Past our empty-nested homes,
    we'll whisper in a hush.

Please help me to remember those years of tinsel past,
When our homes were filled with happy cheers,
We always thought would last.
When getting wakened early on Christmas morn,
Brought them peeking 'round the stairs,
And the pitter patter of little feet
    was something we once shared.

Santa, can you make a snowflake fall gently upon my nose?
Can you bundle me up so warm,
    in all my winter clothes?
Can you take me sledding

down the hill at North Side park?
Santa, can you please bring back
   just a tiny Christmas spark?

Can we unwrap some laughter and some extra fuzzy hugs?
I'll help you warm the cocoa in some extra jumbo mugs!

If you could help me bring back some forgotten memories,
I made a promise to the Christ child
   I'd drop down to my knees.
I'll say a prayer for Christmas peace
   and lend a helping hand,
And ride around the globe with you tonight
   with a message for this land.

Cherish each day as it happens,
put anger and sadness aside,
with the Christ child in the manger,
is where happiness resides.

Santa, I want to say thank you
   for bringing me Christmas cheer.
Jesus, I want to say thank you for calming all my fears.

E. M. Hector

Skinny Santa

I heard a rumor recently—no doubt it has evolved as only rumors do, increasing and changing in its passing—and I feel compelled to do my part in its progression, so I'm passing it along to you.

Someone, somewhere has started a petition to put Santa Claus on a diet.

Can you believe it? His image has faltered. He is no longer deemed a good role model for the youth of today. He is overweight. His unselfish generosity has been over-shadowed by his own mass.

If the facts were known, it would come to light that the very people signing the petition are the ones to blame for his current predicament. What parent has not prompted starry-eyed children to race to the kitchen before bed on Christmas Eve and produce a delightful treat for the year's most anticipated visitor? We are the ones who left the cookies and the milk where he was obligated to acknowl-edge our hospitality by leaving only crumbs and a water ring on the coffee table.

What is the world coming to? The fact that Jolly Old Saint Nick is now considered weight-challenged will shed an entirely new light on the whole Christmas season.

The Night Before Christmas will never be the same:

> *He was chubby and plump, a right jolly old elf,*
> *But now he's taboo, in spite of himself!*

The happy old man in the bright red suit has become a bad influence. Not only does he not eat right, but he obviously doesn't get enough exercise. To make matters worse, he is portrayed as smoking a pipe!

If we're going to town on the old boy, I'd like to call attention to the fact that he's dressed all in fur, from his head to his foot. What self-respecting person, elf or not, would make a fashion statement like that? This should be added to the petition. As well, it is probably inhumane to keep reindeer up all night pulling a heavy, gift-laden sleigh.

Santa needs a new image. He has to get with the program, say the makers of petitions, the guardians of what is right and good.

There is a little child somewhere inside me quivering right now. Wide-eyed, it's watching as the powers-that-be muck with the magic of my favorite time of year. Santa has never been the true meaning of Christmas. He is merely a tool in its delivery. He is the spirit of giving—of secret giving. The faith of children in something they can't fathom. The thanks they give to something unseen.

Sure, Santa could stand to lose a few pounds—so could I. But somehow the vision of a trim St. Nick in red bicycle shorts just doesn't cut it.

Elva Stoelers

4

THE JOY
OF GIVING

Love is, above all, the gift of oneself.

Jean Anouilh

The Greatest Christmas Gift

The sights, the sounds, the treats, the joys!
Yes, Christmas is for girls and boys.
Yet even someone threescore ten
At Christmas is a child again,
Filled with thrills and wild delight
Each and every Christmas night.

I love the stockings, candles, tree,
Songs, and hospitality.
But most of all, I must confess,
I love God's Gift of Righteousness,
Wrapped in a manger filled with hay
And placed in my heart with love to stay—
The greatest Gift of Christmas Day!

Bonnie Compton Hanson

Christmas Spirit

*The only blind person at Christmastime is
he who has not Christmas in his heart.*

Helen Keller

The line of disgruntled customers snaked around the
counter and disappeared somewhere in the menswear
department. There were just two more shopping days
before Christmas, and most of the shoppers in line were in
panic mode, coiling to strike. One of those customers was
my husband, Dale.

Dale is one of those people who shop better under pres-
sure. They are the no-nonsense shoppers who depend on
fast service because every minute counts as the countdown before Christmas continues. But the service here
was anything but fast.

The problem was the elderly lady at the front of the line,
who was twittering happily to the lone salesgirl manning
the cash register.

"This sweater is for my granddaughter," the lady
explained. "She's going to be a teacher, you know. And
she's doing very well. She has a very nice boyfriend who

is an architectural technician. He's just started a job with a good company, but you know, we haven't seen any sign of a ring yet. Young people seem to wait so long these days. They've been going out for quite a while now. Why, I was married with one child and another one on the way when I was her age."

On and on she rattled as she painstakingly counted out her change, oblivious to the writhing serpent of customers behind her. When she finally zipped her purse shut and picked up her parcel, the clerk motioned to the man next in line.

"Thank you, dearie," said the lady as she started to move slowly away, checking the contents of her shopping bag. She was almost to the end of the counter when suddenly she turned back. "Oops! Excuse me," she cried. A collective hiss went down the line. Several fangs were bared. An ominous rattle of keys began in someone's pocket.

"What's this for?" she asked, holding up a piece of paper.

"It's a discount coupon that will give you 15 percent off your next purchase here at the store, from now until the end of January," replied the weary salesgirl.

"Well, thank you, my dear, but I won't be needing this," she beamed. "Here, you can use it right now!" she said, handing it to the man next in line. The man's eyes widened, and he mumbled a word of thanks as she shuffled to the door.

Then an amazing thing happened. The man stepped up to the counter and used the coupon that the elderly lady had given him. When the clerk handed him another coupon for his next visit to the store, he promptly turned around and gave it to the woman in line behind him. After she had used that coupon toward her purchase and the clerk gave her another one, the woman then passed it back to the shopper behind her. By the time it was Dale's turn, the salesclerk had a smile on her face, and so did Dale as he turned around to give his coupon to the lady behind him. And so it went, on down the line until there was nothing left of that disgruntled snake, not even a rattle. One small act of kindness had snowballed into a mountain of goodwill.

Dale says it was one of the best gifts he got that Christmas—when he discovered that the Christmas spirit is still alive and well in our world.

Lisa Beringer

Just One Gift

Gratitude is the memory of the heart.

Jean Baptiste Massieur

It was the only Christmas gift I had ever received, and I remember it still. I was six years old, and my mother handed me the brightly wrapped box, explaining it was from her boss at the office where she worked. I nervously held the package in my lap, almost too afraid to open it. Why had a complete stranger given me a present?

My mother was a single parent and often worked several jobs to make ends meet. There usually wasn't much money left for extras. But that wasn't the reason why we never owned a Christmas tree or any gifts beneath it. I'd never received a Christmas gift because we are Jewish.

"He couldn't believe you didn't have anything to open on Christmas morning," my mother told me. "He wanted me to give this to you."

Although she explained to him that we celebrated Hanukkah and I'd received presents then, he insisted that all children should have a gift to open on Christmas. I could tell she felt uncomfortable, and I did, too. Still, I was only six and couldn't wait to see what was inside.

I carefully unwrapped the box and found a Raggedy Ann doll. Her red yarn hair was soft, and her black button eyes shone. I held her close, and she soon became my favorite toy. I may not have been able to describe the feeling then, but now I know what I felt—it was the Christmas spirit.

Growing up Jewish in a world that celebrates Christmas wasn't always easy. No colorful lights, decorated trees, or trips to see Santa Claus. Our Hanukkah celebrations were fun—lighting the menorah, spinning the dreidel, and having the benefit of eight nights on which to open gifts. Still, each December we were reminded of our differences.

But to my mother's boss, our differences didn't matter. What did matter were the magic of the season and the sharing of joy, and those don't differentiate between Christian and Jewish children. He just wanted to share his joy with me.

So, even though I don't celebrate the holiday, I understand what the Christmas spirit is all about. It doesn't matter what religion you follow, or even what you call it. It's the spirit that prompts people to buy a toy for a child who may not receive any others. It's the spirit that brings Jews into soup kitchens to serve Christmas dinners, or drop coins in a tzedakah box for the needy. It's about sharing your own joy with others, no matter who they are.

I don't remember if I wrote the giver a thank-you note, but I hope I did. More than thirty years later, while I don't know what happened to that doll, I still have the most important gift he gave me—the gift of Christmas spirit.

Ruth Spiro

The Christmas Present

*Perhaps the best Yuletide decoration
is being wreathed in smiles.*

Unknown

"Just four short weeks 'til Christmas!" the radio blared.
I flipped the calendar to December and smiled. In just
three weeks we'd be leaving for Texas to enjoy the festivities with our kids. David and I couldn't wait for the
Christmas cookie bake-off with the grandkids, treating
our ballerina granddaughter to "The Nutcracker," and
seeing the children's delight and wonder of Santa coming down the chimney on Christmas Eve. Presents were
stacking up, ready for wrapping, and then were stuffed
into every nook and cranny of trunk space as our car
headed south.

*Three weeks is a long time to wait to enjoy the spirit of
Christmas,* I thought, looking at the piles of ribbon and
wrapping paper strewn across the dining-room table.
*What can we do here before we leave? The house is much too quiet
without the hubbub of children and the excitement that comes
with their anticipation, yet it makes no sense to put up a tree—*

maybe a wreath on the door. Still, we need to do something more, something special just for the two of us. With that thought, my imagination started to kick in.

The Nebraska winter chill filled the air as David put down his briefcase and slipped through the door that evening. "What's for dinner, Karen? It smells wonderful. Are we having company?"

I greeted David with a kiss and slipped my hand in his, gently leading him into the dining room to receive his first Christmas present.

"It's beautiful, Karen!" he exclaimed. "I love it! But it's only December first!"

The transformed dining-room table, set with the lovely white damask tablecloth handed down from his grand-mother, instantly brought back childhood memories of special dinners in David's grandparents' home—just as I knew it would. The sterling silver flatware given to my mother as a wedding gift graced two place settings of our fine white china adorned with deep green salad plates and matching colored-glass stemware. Monogrammed sterling napkin slides given to David's mother and father by his grandparents added the finishing touch to the nap-kins. The flickering flames of the candles cast shadows on the silver candelabra and the glimmering silver serving pieces we took pleasure in discovering together on our antique treasure hunts.

"We're starting a new Christmas tradition," I said. "With only the two of us and no family close by, I'd like to make the holiday special, just for us. Whether we have a five-course dinner or a simple bowl of soup, we're going to enjoy it with all the trimmings all month long!"

Embracing me in his arms, David grinned. "You know what a hopeless romantic I am, Karen. This is the best Christmas present you could have ever given me!"

As we sat down to enjoy our intimate rendezvous,

strains of Handel's "Messiah" filled the air, reminding us of the best Christmas present ever given—the gift of God's unconditional love wrapped in the person of his son, Jesus.

Karen R. Kilby

Six Brown Eggs

The joy of brightening others' lives,
bearing each other's burdens, easing other's
loads, and supplanting empty hearts and
lives with generous gifts, becomes for
us the magic of Christmas.

W. C. Jones

It was the Great Depression. My father and two of his younger brothers were wool growers in southern Utah. The bottom had dropped out of the wool business, as it also had for cattle and sheep. There was no money. We could neither sell anything nor buy anything.

Papa was almost always at the sheep camp, even at Thanksgiving and Christmas. And since our mother had died when the youngest sister was born, we children were alone. Year after year, we took care of ourselves. We planned our own Thanksgivings and Christmases. But we missed our father. We felt things were not quite fair.

This year, one of his brothers said he would relieve our father at the sheep herd. Our father, our dear papa, would be home! We were overcome with joy. We planned all the things we could do for our marvelous Christmas!

My sisters, Melba, Emma, and little Verle, dragged out the bedraggled Christmas decorations and made the house festive. Jesse cut and stacked armloads of wood on the back porch. He killed a fat hen and left her hanging to drain and freeze. I would dress her for Christmas dinner. I saved the eggs. The hens seldom laid eggs in the cold winter, so I saved every one to make custard pies for Papa. Papa loved custard pies.

Then we learned that Papa's brother did not go to the sheep herd. He was home with his family, as always. Papa would not be home. Christmas lost its meaning. There was no money and no way of getting any to buy presents. We had made so many happy plans. For a few moments, our world seemed to fall apart.

At fifteen, I was the oldest. My sisters looked at me with wondering eyes—eyes that said, "Jennie, can't you do something? Won't we have any kind of Christmas?"

I went to the pantry to hide my tears. Inside were the six brown eggs; I just looked at them. Then I looked again at these big, brown Barred Rock eggs. Eggs were as scarce as money. Why, those eggs were valuable! They were a dollar, a whole dollar! I laid them carefully on a folded towel in the brass kettle.

My sisters stared at me as I put on my coat and hood, and pulled on my overshoes. They saw my beaming face, and their faces brightened. "Be careful with the fire," I said at the door, "but keep it going. Santa Claus is at the store, and I'm going to see him."

I ran like the wind, plowing through snow that came over the top of my overshoes. What if the stores were all closed? "Oh, dear Heavenly Father," I prayed, "please, please help me."

The stores were dark. All the storekeepers and the clerks had gone home. But then—a flicker of light in Leo

Munson's store sparked my hopes. I literally fell through the door as Leo opened it to go home. I held on to the eggs, and, miraculously, none of them were broken.

Leo looked at the eggs, then at me holding the bucket out to him and trying to explain why I was there. I heard myself blurting, "Christmas, Leo, for Jesse and my little sisters. This is all I have. Are they—are they worth a dollar?"

Leo understood, probably far more than I knew. "Don't say another word, Jennie," he said. "A dollar! I haven't been able to buy an egg in town. No one will sell any. My wife wants eggs for Christmas."

He got sacks and put the things we needed most in them: gloves, socks, stockings. He filled the sacks up even with some store candy and five big, beautiful oranges. "One of those oranges is for you, Jennie," he said. "Merry Christmas!"

I thanked Leo and thanked him again. Then, with those big, full sacks, I stumbled out the door.

There was no deep snow, no cold wind, no ice, nor sagging, cracking trees. Violets were blooming, and birds were singing, and I walked on apple blossoms. Home to Christmas, bought with six brown eggs—and some help from Leo Munson.

Jennie Spencer Baty

The Treasured Gifts Come Without Ribbons or Bows

*P*eace on Earth will come to stay, when
we live Christmas every day.

Helen Steiner Rice

"Sometimes the best gifts come without ribbons or bows," Grandma always told us before telling us this favorite family story.

It was 1918, and Grandpa had gone to work paving the roadways and laying railroad tracks in the city while Grandma was working part-time in the canneries. When Papa came home from work, he'd eat a hurried supper and then rush off to night school to get his education. After Grandpa graduated and attained his American citizenship, he went to work full-time on the cannery lines and part-time in a shoe-repair shop. He labored on the night shift so that his days would be free to take care of the children, thereby allowing Grandma to attend school and receive an education.

Grandma anticipated her first day of school in America.

The day of her first class was a very important moment in her young life. She knew that she needed an education to become a good citizen of her new country.

On the morning of her first class, Grandma excitedly rushed to dress for school. Though she didn't have much of a wardrobe, what she did own was clean and well-pressed. As she slipped her feet into her best pair of long black stockings, Grandma's happy mood dissolved into somber sadness as she discovered her only pair of black stockings riddled with gaping holes.

"Forget about your socks, Mama. You haven't time to mend them now," urged Grandpa. "You'll be late for class. And, anyway, I have a surprise for you!"

A moment later, Grandpa handed Grandma her old high-button shoes. Only now she hardly recognized her old shoes—they gleamed with brand-new leather soles and shiny black laces. She could see her reflection in their brilliant shine. While she had slept that night, Grandpa secretly worked until the wee hours to repair Grandma's old high-button shoes.

Grandma's eyes welled with tears of gratitude as she placed a kiss on her husband's cheek. "I will look like a fine lady in these wonderful shoes, Papa," she said.

"Hurry now, Mama, hurry. Slip your feet inside these beautiful shoes, and no one will ever suspect you have holey stockings. It will be our little secret," Grandpa promised.

Grandma had no time now to mend her tattered stockings. So, she did as her husband suggested and slipped her stockinged feet into her high-button shoes. She quickly laced them up and rushed out the doorway, pausing only a moment for Grandpa to kiss her good-bye and hand her two one-dollar bills for her classroom tuition.

Arriving at school that morning, Grandma felt uneasy in a classroom filled with strangers. Standing at the head of the class was a stern-looking teacher by the name of Miss Peabody. In her hand she held a long, ominous-looking pointer stick, which she used both for pointing and intimidation.

That morning, Miss Peabody passed a large empty bowl around the classroom and instructed each student to drop the tuition fees into the container. Every student complied. One of the more affluent students paid his fee with a bright two-dollar gold piece.

After collecting all the money, the teacher placed the bowl on her desk. Later that afternoon, when Miss Peabody tallied up the tuition money, she discovered the gold coin was missing. Convinced that one of her students took the gold piece, she demanded that everyone in the classroom empty their pockets on her desk. The students promptly obeyed, but no gold coin appeared.

Angry and frustrated, the teacher took her search one step farther and demanded that everyone in the classroom remove his or her shoes. A small gold coin could easily hide in the rim of a high-button shoe.

One by one, the students removed their shoes—everyone, that is, except Grandma. She sat there frozen with embarrassment, hoping and praying the missing coin would turn up before she had to slip off her shoes. But a few minutes later, when the coin failed to appear, Miss Peabody pointed her stick directly at Grandma's shoes and demanded she remove them.

For what seemed like an eternity, the entire classroom stared down at Grandma's feet. Grandma, who had been so proud of her elegant shoes, just couldn't remove them now in front of her peers and expose her holey stockings. To do so would be a great disgrace.

Grandma's reluctance to remove her shoes convinced the teacher of her guilt. Miss Peabody marched Grandma off to the principal's office. Grandma, in tears, immediately telephoned Grandpa, who rushed down to the school. Grandpa explained to the principal why his wife was reluctant to remove her shoes.

The understanding principal then allowed Grandma to remove her shoes in the privacy of his office. He soon discovered the only thing Grandma was hiding was a pair of unsightly, tattered stockings.

Grandma returned to her classroom, but all that day a shadow of suspicion hung over her.

Late that afternoon, just before the dismissal bell, Grandma was completely exonerated of any wrongdoing. When her teacher, Miss Peabody, raised her right arm to write the class assignment on the blackboard, the missing coin fell from the cuff of her sleeve and rolled across the room in plain view of the entire classroom. Earlier that day, when the teacher had counted up the money, the stiffly starched cuff of her dress had accidentally scooped up the small coin.

That afternoon, when Grandma returned home from school, Papa was waiting for her on the front porch swing. Exhausted from his night job, he was quietly napping. Cradled in his hardworking hands was Grandma's darning basket. Inside the basket were all of Grandma's old stockings that Grandpa had carefully and lovingly mended.

In later years, Grandpa prospered as a a successful businessman. He took special pride in giving his wife stockings made from the finest silks and woolens. Though Grandma appreciated these fine gifts, she often said they were never so dear to her, or so well loved, as those old tattered stockings, so lovingly mended by her husband's calloused, hardworking hands.

Cookie Curci

Papa's Radio

From home to home, and
heart to heart, from one place to another.
The warmth and joy of Christmas
brings us closer to each other.

Emily Matthews

As a young Italian-American, my childhood was filled with stories that boasted colorful characters, lively dialogue, and wonderful settings. But, best of all, each story taught me a valuable lesson. Children's storybooks, you say? No. Although I did my share of reading fanciful, illustrated fairy tales and nursery rhymes, the stories that filled my childhood were not written down. They were spoken.

Night after night, as I lay in bed with a soft, hand-stitched quilt drawn up under my chin, I listened in the dark as my mother, my father, a grandparent, a visiting uncle, or an older cousin would fill the nighttime silence with stories of life in the old country—Italy. Or even tell stories of life in the new country—America.

I loved these family tales. Each one gave me a clearer picture of my ancestors or a better understanding of the relatives I already knew. One of my favorite nighttime stories was of Grandpa and his beloved radio, and how it helped him learn the real meaning of friendship.

Papa Vincenzo nestled comfortably into his rocker and, with a twist of his hand, clicked on the dial of his brand-new RCA Victor radio. It was Papa's habit each night, after one of Mama Saveria's robust Italian meals, to position himself by his beloved radio and tune in the nightly antics of radio characters: "Fibber McGee and Molly," "Amos 'n Andy," "Edgar Bergen and Charlie McCarthy," and "The Lone Ranger."

There were no complexities to Papa Vincenzo's lifestyle; his needs were easily satisfied by a good meal, a warm home, and a loving family. He lived his life by the simple and old-fashioned creed: "Pray for the things you want; work for the things you need."

If Papa had one luxury, it was the acquisition of a household radio. The radio had become a vital component of his daily life. It restored his energy and brought back his sense of humor after a long workday in the fruit orchards of the Santa Clara Valley. With the impending arrival of World War II, the economy had begun to tighten, but my budget-wise Grandpa had managed to scrimp and save enough money from his meager earnings as a tree pruner to purchase the new radio. Although Papa had known poverty in the Old Country, he felt he'd never been poor, only broke. Being poor, Papa believed, was a state of mind; being broke was only a temporary situation.

Papa loved his new radio, but Grandma preferred listening to her old Victrola or puttering around her wood stove to sitting by the radio—until the day she heard her first episode of "One Man's Family" on NBC radio. From that moment on, she was an ardent fan of the new media.

In time, Grandma came to believe the radio had been sent to them as a blessing. It helped both her and Papa Vincenzo to learn better English, and it boosted their social life as well. The radio gave them a common topic to discuss with their neighbors, who also listened nightly to the same radio programs.

On warm summer nights, Papa's neighborhood cronies, Mr. Goldstein, Mr. Miller, and Mr. Rosenberg, sat with Papa on his front stoop, discussing their favorite radio programs. There were times when Mr. Goldstein explained the meaning of a certain Yiddish word Papa had heard on the "Molly Goldberg Show." Other times, Papa translated a Puccini opera for Mr. Goldstein. Some nights, the old friends had a good laugh at the expense of the contestants on "Major Bowes' Original Amateur Hour." The radio helped to bond these old friends, who came from vastly different backgrounds, in a way few things could. The men had left their Old Country to escape tyranny and oppression, and as young immigrants they had settled into the neighborhood together. Although they came from varied parts of the world and followed different religious beliefs, the old friends shared a love for their new country and family traditions.

And so their friendship grew—until that fateful December day in 1941, when Papa's radio brought him the terrible news that Pearl Harbor had been attacked. He would hear President Roosevelt declare war with Japan and the Axis powers, Germany and Italy. It was a declaration of war that changed Papa's life.

The knock on Papa's door came early that December morning in 1941. It brought with it a special-delivery letter from the government of the United States declaring that Papa must surrender all radios on his premises—effective immediately!

Papa Vincenzo had no political ties to his former country.

He had worked and lived in America for more than thirty years and raised his children and grandchildren as honest, hardworking American citizens. But the fact remained that he was a native of Italy, a country now ruled by the fascist tyrant Benito Mussolini, who chose to side with the Axis powers against the United States.

As Papa read the dispatch, tears of indignation rolled down his face. Losing his radio would be sad enough, but Papa was more concerned that he might lose the company and respect of his friends in the community, which he had earned for more than thirty years.

More than anything else, Papa prided himself on his honest and high moral character. He was a man of his word. Now he feared that a war thousands of miles away had cast a shadow of aspersions over him. It appeared Papa's fears were well-founded; some of his employers, leery of Italian aliens, started canceling their job offers. Papa worried that his longtime friendship with the Goldsteins, the Rosenbergs, and the Millers was also in jeopardy. Would they also view him differently now? Could they somehow believe he shared the same political views and beliefs as the terrible tyrant Mussolini?

That Christmas Eve, in 1941, Papa and Grandma sat quietly in their favorite chairs, warming themselves by the fire. Papa couldn't help but miss the raucous sounds of his radio, and the daily banter with his friends and neighbors, which he feared he had now lost.

A knock on the door brought Papa quickly to his feet. He approached his front door with trepidation. Opening the door, Papa was relieved and surprised to find the warm familiar faces of his old pals standing on his front stoop.

Mr. Goldstein was the first to speak up. "Vincenzo, my friend, the United States government says that you can no longer own a radio. Is this correct?"

Wearing a quizzical expression on his face, Papa answered, "Yes—yes, this is so."

"But the government did not forbid you should listen to the radio, correct?" inquired Mr. Rosenberg.

"Correct," Papa repeated.

Papa's neighbors handed him a sheet of paper, on which was written a handwritten time schedule listing all of his favorite radio programs. Each program and time corresponded with a neighbor's address. His old pals had gotten together and worked out a radio listening schedule for Papa and Grandma that included every show from "The Goldbergs" to "Little Orphan Annie."

"Read it, my friend," encouraged Mr. Rosenberg. "It's all there. On Monday, you and the missus will listen to 'Fibber McGee and Molly' at the Millers' home; on Tuesday, 'The Goldbergs' and 'Major Bowes Show' at my house; on Wednesday, 'Edgar Bergen and Charlie McCarthy' at the Smiths' house, and so on, until all of your favorite programs are accounted for. You and the missus won't miss one of your favorite shows if we can help it, Vincenzo."

Papa's eyes welled with tears, but this time they were tears of joy and gratitude. Papa invited his dear friends into his house to celebrate the occasion. While Papa poured a glass of his homemade red wine for each of his friends, Grandma passed around her freshly baked biscotti.

Before going to bed that night, Papa and Grandma said a special silent prayer of thanks. Papa had lost his valuable radio on that somber day in 1941, but what he'd found in friendship on that very special Christmas Eve was truly priceless.

The great Chinese philosopher Lao Tzu wrote, "Kindness in words creates confidence, kindness in thinking creates profoundness, but kindness in sharing creates love."

Cookie Curci

Elvis Was Wrong!

My lip quivered as I heard Elvis croon "I'll Be Home for Christmas" on the car radio. Christmas was two weeks away, and this year my husband and I would be spending it alone. In August, the military sent my daughter and her husband, along with my two grandchildren, to a Navy base in Japan to serve our country. We had always shared Christmas with them, but this year our house would be empty. No one was coming home for Christmas, and I was miserable.

This was the daughter who had made me cry when I found out I was pregnant again. I fussed, fumed, and ranted at my fate. I had just given birth three months earlier to her brother, and I didn't think I was ready for another child so soon.

Nine months later, a blonde-haired girl with blue eyes the size of saucers stole my heart. Over the years, we forged a bond tighter than Super Glue. Every year on her birthday, I thanked God for my gift.

Now, she was temporarily gone from my life. Every day was hard, and the Christmas season was excruciating. Lights, gifts, family love—they all reminded me of my daughter. Her smile lit up a room, her gift of generosity was boundless, and her love for her family and friends was immense. I missed her so much that my heart ached.

Earlier that day, my husband had phoned me at work to make sure I was coming straight home.

"Gotta get that tree tonight. Only two weeks left," he stated solemnly.

"Sure thing, babe. We'll go tonight," I said, halfheartedly.

Bah, humbug! I thought. I didn't want a tree or presents or lights or anything that reminded me I wasn't going to share Christmas with my daughter. That night after work, I pulled into our garage and trudged into the house.

"Hi, honey, I'm home!" I yelled.

There was no answer. As I walked through the hall, I noticed a glow coming from the living room. I stepped into the room to see a fully decorated Christmas tree standing in the far corner. Sitting on the floor in front of the tree was my daughter and her family.

"Merry Christmas!" they all yelled in unison. On the couch sat my husband, grinning from ear to ear, enjoying his part in pulling off the coup.

"You didn't think I'd miss Christmas with you, did you, Mom?" she said, jumping up to give me a giant hug. Those big blue eyes were bright with tears.

"This is the second best present ever," I whispered, my voice choking with emotion. "The best gift was when you came into my life," I said, squeezing her back.

The next moment I was engulfed in a group hug. The entire family joined in a heartwarming moment and a memory for many Christmases to come.

Sallie A. Rodman

A Christmas Moment

It was 1997. I sat at my dining-room table and wondered how I would ever get ready for Christmas. I was tired and weak, and every muscle and nerve in my body were screaming.

I looked out my window to see the sun shining and the grass still semigreen. It was already December 20, and this was Minnesota. We were wishing for snow!

Without getting up from my chair at home, I knew people all over the world were scurrying to finish their last-minute preparations for Christmas. And then there was me. I was just beginning to do what most people had already accomplished.

I decided right then that I would put my physical pain aside and treat myself to a little outing, even if I was behind in preparations. Christmas would still arrive.

After convincing my husband that his John Deere suspenders and dingy-looking cap were unacceptable at the theater, we headed to A Center for the Arts, our local art theater. We were treated to one of the finest hours of Christmas entertainment ever by Lance Johnson at the Mighty Wurlitzer.

The music swirled about me as he commanded the keys and the pedals to the sounds of trains, bells, drums, chimes, and music boxes. Memories flooded my soul as "Silent Night," "The Birthday of a King," and "White Christmas" were performed in all their splendor.

Shortly after we had taken our seats, an elderly gentleman with a cane sat down with some difficulty in the low and somewhat narrow theater seat ahead of us. I'd had difficulty myself. He removed his hat—like any gentleman would do—and then proceeded to eat his brown bag lunch, which he had brought with him. This was okay by me. I, too, needed a Diet Coke in my hand, even though I had gallantly resisted the powerful and tempting aroma of the theater popcorn.

His head, with a crown of white hair, began to bob in time to the beat of the music. Although I could not see his feet, I knew they were tapping also, as I saw his knee rising up and down in rhythm. I wondered about his own story. Who was this gentle old man who had come alone to treat himself to a bit of Christmas spirit? Where did he live? What were his memories? Was he married? Perhaps his wife was in a nursing home now, or perhaps she had passed away many Christmases ago. Where were his children or his grandchildren, and would they be joining him to celebrate the holidays?

I watched him eat his sandwich as he carefully wiped his mouth with his napkin, and I wondered how many miles he used to have to walk on his way to school. Did he farm or maintain a business—or perhaps he taught or preached? My thoughts danced in time to the music as I wondered if he had experienced the old-fashioned sleigh rides, or perhaps it was even his only means of getting to the small country church on Christmas Eve. I wondered if he had believed in Santa Claus as a child or had eaten hard Christmas candy and peanuts in the shell. I wondered if he had ever performed as Joseph at the manger in a Christmas play, a lowly shepherd guarding his flocks by night, or one of the wise men who were following the star and seeking the child.

The last song heralded from the Mighty Wurlitzer as it disappeared into the stage. The old man clapped his hands with appreciation of the performance, as we all did. Our hearts were filled with great joy!

The lights came on, and I watched him struggle to get out of the low, small theater seat. I struggled from the seat behind him and gently, but firmly took a hold of his arm and lifted as he rose to his feet. He turned to my husband, who was already standing in the aisle, and said, "Thank you."

It occurred to me that he didn't know that the little boost had come from me. And that's the joy of Christmas—doing something for someone and not needing acknowledgment for it or expecting something in return. Christmas truly arrived to the old man and me in that moment. The cards and the baking and the hurry-scurry melted into oblivion. The beauty, magic, and joy of the season were captured instead. I was now ready for Christmas. And I was five days early!

Glorianne Swenson

Christmas Lost—and Found

Christmas waves a magic wand over this world,
and behold, everything is softer and more beautiful.

Norman Vincent Peale

I remember standing alone in the darkness and humidity on the rear balcony of our fourth-floor apartment, leaning on the railing. The faint odor of curry and jasmine drifted up as I gazed over the gently rustling palm trees toward the blackness of the Arabian Sea beyond. It was Christmas Eve 1960, and I was in Bombay, India, where my foreign-service family was stationed.

My two younger sisters and brother were excited—it was Christmas after all! But I was fifteen, and to me nothing was right. Christmas was my favorite holiday, but as much as I tried, I just couldn't get into the spirit.

I brushed my sweaty hair from my forehead and looked around. Most people in Bombay did not celebrate Christmas. There were no outdoor displays in the neighborhood. No windows glowed with trees covered in multicolored lights. The downtown maze of narrow streets, bicycles, and people contained no department stores, and the crowded, one-room shops run by local merchants were never decorated. From the radio came only wavering Indian music, not the well-known songs of Christmas. And as for the heartwarming, happy-ending Christmas stories we now enjoy on television each year, well, television had not yet come to Bombay.

Turning around, I saw our "tree" in the living room behind me. We had one of the few artificial trees sold in Bombay. It was a skinny thing, its wire branches barely covered with shredded green cellophane. Even the decorations we had brought from the States couldn't fill it out. It was a tree Charlie Brown would surely have appreciated.

I sighed. I was homesick and felt more than a little sorry for myself. I longed for the cold, the smell of pine, and the magic of Christmases past.

Then, as a warm breeze drifted through the open windows, I thought I heard music. I held my breath and listened more closely. It sounded like Christmas carols. But here in India?

The music grew louder as I rushed through the apartment to the front balcony. In the courtyard below, lit by the splashing fountain and surrounded by flowers, a dozen people were singing carols. They wore colorful cotton saris and sandals instead of woolen coats and boots. They probably had never felt the chill of a bitter, winter wind and, even more likely, had probably never seen snow. But their voices rose in harmony to where I stood, filling the air with the comfort of the familiar songs of "Silent Night," "Jingle Bells," and finally, "I'm Dreaming of a White Christmas."

I never found out where they came from, and I doubt they ever knew the difference their singing made, but on that hot December night, they brought a special gift— they returned Christmas to a lonely fifteen-year-old far away from home.

Michele Ivy Davis

The Doll in Burgundy Twill

*What is Christmas? It is tenderness
for the past, courage for the present, hope
for the future. It is a fervent wish that every cup
may overflow, with blessings rich and eternal,
and that every path may lead to peace.*

Agnes M. Pharo

We had a tree that year—smaller than usual, from the back of the tree lot. But it was our Christmas tree. My three younger sisters and I helped Mom lug it home through the snow-crusted streets of our south Philadelphia neighborhood.

Even though I was mature for a ten-year-old, I had no idea of the reality of our situation. School was out for Christmas vacation—two weeks of pure childhood pleasure: baking sugar cookies, playing in the snow, starry-eyed daydreaming of Christmas presents, and the New Year's celebration at Grandmom's house.

We hadn't seen or heard from Daddy in months. After three years of being in and out of our lives, he'd finally left for good. At ten, you don't realize how big the hole in your heart is from abandonment. But you do feel the emptiness even though the house is inhabited by four chatty, arguing, giggling little girls and their devoted mother.

Mom stood the tree in its stand and set out the boxes of ornaments.

"I want a Betsy Wetsy doll," Tootsie, my three-year-old sister, said.

"I want roller skates," six-year-old Diane piped up.

"A bike," Rosanne said. She would turn eight in just a month.

"You know the city isn't a good place for bike riding," Mom said. "It's too dangerous. Here. Hang this gold ball, honey."

"What do you want, Mom?" I asked, hoping she would say Evening in Paris cologne. I'd saved up the dimes I had earned helping Aunt Rosie with chores and bought the blue-bottled set of talc and cologne at Sun Ray Drugs a week earlier. I couldn't wait for Mom to open it.

"I have everything I want," Mom smiled. "I have four beautiful daughters."

The tree turned out to be as lovely as we had hoped. The bubble lights, sparkling glass balls, and silver tinsel filled in the empty spaces between branches. On Christmas Eve, we hopped into bed, anxious for morning to come. Toots and Diane listened for hooves on the rooftop of our three-story brick row home. Eventually, we all talked ourselves to sleep.

"Get up! Get up! It's Christmas!" Diane shook us and ran into Mom's room while the first rays of winter sunshine still slept below the horizon.

"Wait here until I put the tree lights on," Mom instructed, pulling on her chenille robe. Everything had to be just right.

We stood at the top of the stairs in slippers and flannel pajamas until we got the okay, then down the steps we bounded. One at a time, Mom handed out the gifts—wrapped packages of underwear (of course) for everybody, our own socks stuffed with oranges and nuts, and one special present each. With delight, I held the doll dressed in a rich burgundy twill coat and hat.

"Oh, Mom, she's beautiful," I said.

"Don't you recognize her?" Mom asked.

Puzzled, I shook my head.

"It's your old doll. I made her a new outfit."

I looked at the peaches-and-cream face with blue glass eyes. It was, indeed, my old doll all dressed up. Her new attire made her look brand-new.

"Mom, I love it!"

Tootsie's old doll rested in a mushroom-box bassinet outfitted with handmade bedding. Rosanne and Diane opened similar presents. As I watched, a deeper understanding of our circumstances grew, and a deeper respect for Mom grew along with it. I beamed when she oohed and aahed over the Evening in Paris, filled with joy that I could bless her with something special.

That was many years ago. Mom is at home with the Lord, and I'm a grandma now. But as I look back at all the Christmases that have come and gone, this special one stands out above the rest. I realize now how brokenhearted my mother must have been when her little girls voiced their Christmas wishes. How she must have wracked her brain to come up with suitable gifts for each child at little or no cost.

I never told her. Now I wish I had. But the old doll dressed in handcrafted, love-inspired burgundy twill is the gift I will always remember most.

Emily King

God and Santa

"Rachel's lost her doll," Dody told the Bible study group one evening. "Would you guys pray about it?"

Rachel's doll had been inherited from her older sisters, a Christmas present several years before. Now, at six, Rachel carried Abby everywhere except to kindergarten. She slept with Abby, talked to Abby, and explained things to Abby. Rachel was especially impressed by the fact that this particular Cabbage Patch doll had hair the same color and style as hers and had a particularly nice expression.

The family—Daddy, Mommy, Rachel, and, of course, Abby—dined out one evening. They were halfway home when a cry sounded from the backseat.

"Daddy! You have to go back! Abby's not here!"

Dody phoned the restaurant and described the doll and where they had been sitting. The manager was friendly, but no one had turned in a doll.

Rachel cried herself to sleep that night.

After sending her red-eyed little girl off to school, Dody drove back to the restaurant, even crawling under the table to be sure. No Abby.

"Rachel is positive Santa will give Abby back to her this Christmas," Dody told us. "But I've checked in all the toy stores. They don't make the dolls with that color hair any-more! Bob went online, hoping to buy one. I told Rachel that Santa might give her another doll, a different one. But she is positive that she will get her 'real' Abby."

Dody sighed.

I asked why Rachel knew she'd get Abby back, and Dody told me she had prayed about it. "'God answers prayers, right, Mommy?' she told me. We've talked about how sometimes God says no, but she is convinced God and Santa will return Abby to her. So, would you all pray about this? And if you know anyone with a Cabbage Patch doll with long, brown hair. . . ."

* * *

"Good morning, Mom!"

"G'morning, dear!" Sue returned her daughter's kiss, gave the eggs one last stir, and handed her a plate. "Bacon's in the oven."

"Thanks, Mom!"

"I was just thinking," Sue said slowly, "about your dolls."

"My dolls?" Ricki laughed. "Come on, Mom! I'm in high school and don't play with dolls anymore."

"What did you do with your dolls?" her mother asked.

"Well, I wanted to give them away," Ricki said, "but you wanted me to keep them. So they're all in boxes, in the back of the closet downstairs. Why?"

"Rachel lost her doll." Sue told her the story. "Didn't you have one with brown hair?"

"Yep!" Ricki recalled. "I think I do have that doll! I've gotta run, Mom, but would you check? That would be so neat!"

Ricki set her plate in the sink, kissed her mother good-bye, and headed out, giving one last wave as her convert-ible turned out of the driveway.

Sue finished her own breakfast more slowly, then went downstairs to look for those dolls.

* * *

"Mommy, look!"

Dody had been picking up bits of ribbon and wrapping paper, waiting for her daughter to get to that one special package under the tree.

"Look!" Rachel called again. "It's Abby! Oh, Abby, I've missed you so! Why did you go away so long?"

She cradled the doll in her arms, her face aglow.

"I told you Santa would give her back to me!" Rachel ran to her mother to display the precious toy. "'Cause I asked God to tell him to."

"Thank you, God!" She hugged the doll close. "Thanks for letting Santa give Abby back to me!"

Rachel spun around a couple of times, then held Abby at arms' length to admire her.

"You've got a new dress," she announced. "And, Mommy, while Abby was gone, visiting Santa, she grew a tooth! Mommy, this is the best Christmas ever!"

* * *

"That was the best Christmas," Dody told us at Bible study a few weeks later. "Loss is part of life, so she could have dealt with never seeing Abby again. But she was so confident that God was going to help her! I didn't want that faith shaken."

She looked over at Sue and smiled.

"I can't thank you enough," she said. "It was so nice of Ricki to give Rachel her doll!"

"Ricki loves Rachel," Sue said, "and she had fun dressing the doll for her and sneaking it to you for Christmas. Isn't it funny that we would have the exact doll you needed?"

"That's not funny," someone said. "That's grace!"

A few years passed. Rachel was in second grade, still sleeping with Abby. Ricki was starting college. Dody invited Sue and Ricki over for supper one night.

"I liked the pie," Rachel agreed. "Ricki, Mommy said you gave me Abby back. Will you tell me the story?"

"How did you lose Abby in the first place?" Ricki asked when they were seated in the living room, with the fire crackling quietly.

"We were at the restaurant, eating french fries," Rachel explained. "Abby was sitting in the corner. But when we got home, she wasn't there! Then, on Christmas, there she was, with a tooth!"

Everyone laughed.

"We wrote our phone number under her head, see? So she'd never get lost again," Rachel went on, her doll securely in her lap. "Was Abby your special doll?"

"No, but I had another doll I loved best. When I saw you after Christmas, you told me all about how Santa had given Abby back to you! It was neat to see my old doll being used again. That was fun for me and made it a special Christmas!"

Rachel leaned over to kiss Abby, then looked up. "It was a good Christmas when I got Abby. And a really good Christmas when I got her back! But, you know something? It's the best Christmas to know that God knew Ricki had my doll and answered my prayer!"

Rachel gave Ricki a big hug, and both girls beamed at Abby, loved and safe in Rachel's arms.

Elsi Dodge

The Twelve Days of Christmas

*To give and then not to feel that one has given
is the very best of all ways of giving.*

Max Beerbohm

It was Christmas. The snow that gently hugged the tips of the mountains and the *farolitos* (paper lanterns) that graced the homes and business establishments in the desert Southwest told me so. But it was not Christmas in my heart. My children were busy with their holiday parties, and simply baking the perfunctory cookies for them was a massive chore. You see, tragedy had struck our family just four months earlier by way of the untimely and sad death of my oldest daughter, Kristen.

Much to my surprise, life proceeded, albeit on a surreal level. *How would I get through the holidays? How could I be strong for my family?*

Christmas was just two weeks away, and my parents decided to fly out and join us. They had not weathered the death of their grandchild well. It was good that we would all be together for this holiday. Little did we know what was about to happen to us on that holiday.

It was a quiet night. The lights of Albuquerque sparkled below us, and I had just finished playing Christmas songs on my piano when the front doorbell chimed. My son, Nick, was quick to see who had come to visit us this late. "What in the world?" he exclaimed. "There is no one here." My daughter, Kate, ran to the door and gasped in surprise. Sitting on the front porch was a beautiful white candle covered in a glass dome. The fire of the candle danced merrily, and we quickly brought it inside. How nice! Who could have given us such a nice present? Why didn't they stay so that we could thank them? So many questions!

The following night, after a particularly stressful day, we once again heard the sound of the doorbell. The children laughed merrily. This time, a basket of freshly baked ginger cookies was left for us. They were still warm and covered with a clean red-checkered dishtowel. Nick quickly ran out onto the porch and into the driveway. No one was there.

What was going on? Who could be doing this? And how could they disappear so quickly without a trace into the night?

On the third night, we waited with anticipation. Nick had a plan that he felt would be foolproof. He would be ready this time if the doorbell rang. He camped out in the foyer, directly in front of the door. Sure enough, this time, there came a knock. Before anyone had a chance to respond, Nick swung open the door. However, much to his chagrin, he wasn't fast enough. Nestled among delicate green foil were two crystal tree ornaments. They were filled with a fragrant, spicy potpourri. We immediately placed them in a prominent location on our Christmas tree. This was fun! My father's eyes sparkled with life, and my mother's face was lit with a happy smile. How wonderful! Someone was playing the "Twelve Days of Christmas" on us. But who? Who could be doing such a wonderful thing?

The fourth night arrived, accompanied by a storm. Wind and snow lapped against our windows with a fury, and we were certain we would not receive a visit from our Christmas Ghost on such a dreary and cold night. We were wrong! Right on schedule, the front door rattled with a knock, and this time, two tiny, wooden angels with starched lace wings were left behind for us to behold. The children ran to the end of the porch. Nothing could be seen, not even a footprint in the snow. Such a mystery!

On the fifth, sixth, and seventh nights, we received tall, honey wax candles, a nut bread bursting with cherries and almonds, and a tiny nutcracker carved from clothes-pins and held together with pipe cleaners, Now it was time to get down to serious business. Our curiosity was piqued. We simply had to know our mystery benefactor.

"No," said my father. "Whoever it is does not want to be seen, and it is our responsibility to keep it that way. This is part of the gift. This angel is also receiving a gift, the pure and obvious joy of giving, secure in the knowledge that he or she is bringing joy to this family at a very diffi-cult time."

He, of course, was right.

On the eighth night, we waited. No one came. Disappointed and tired, we went to bed. We had come to look forward to our nocturnal visits and now wondered why they had stopped. Morning dawned brightly, and when my husband stepped outside to retrieve his paper, lo and behold! On our threshold were two gifts: a red poinsettia, and a lovely Christmas cactus that was prepar-ing to bloom. Our friend had truly caught us off guard this time. Indeed, our eighth and ninth day gifts had been quietly left outside our door sometime during the night.

On the tenth night, we received an apple pie, steaming hot and carefully wrapped in red and green napkins. On the eleventh day, brown and white handmade coasters made of cardboard and lined with satin ribbon were left. So lovely!

Christmas Eve was upon us, and it had happened so quickly that we forgot our sad spirit. Our sweet angel had taken our minds from our loss and had treated us to a very different kind of Christmas. It was one that we had never anticipated. Each night, the children had run outside in a vain effort to catch a glimpse of our benevolent friends, and yet, on the twelfth night, we still had no idea who had so diligently and kindly bestowed us with its sweet blessings.

On the twelfth day—Christmas Day—we sat in the living room. All of our gifts had been exchanged, and we had enjoyed a quiet family dinner. It had been a good Christmas, after all, loving and joyous. Then, as usual, the front doorbell rang. Right on cue, our secret Santa disappeared into the night, leaving behind a small white envelope. Upon opening it, we found that our twelfth Christmas gift was a message, neatly written in a child's hand. It read:

> I am the spirit of Christmas
> Which is PEACE
> I am the spirit of gladness—HOPE
> I am the heart of Christmas, which is LOVE
> Have a Merry Christmas!

We were changed from that night on. We began to heal. Going on with our lives seemed a bit easier. We never knew who left all of those wonderful gifts. We did, however, divine the "Spirit of Christmas" and how important it is to take the time for friends. We learned how essential it is to bring a bit of sunshine into a dark place, not simply at Christmas, but all year through.

Janet K. Brennan

The Gift of Normandy Beach

Christmas is not a date.
It is a state of mind.

Mary Ellen Chase

It was our last day in Paris. Instead of touring the Eiffel Tower or admiring the Mona Lisa, my husband and I were careening down dark alleys. With a lurch, the minivan merged with the northbound stream of traffic for a two-and-a-half-hour drive to the sea.

This tour was an afterthought. The day before, I had noticed a brochure in the hotel lobby advertising a complete tour of the D-Day invasion. Tim's dad and uncle had both been at D-Day. I thought this would be something special for him. Since the excursion was offered only once a week, we had to act quickly.

"It's too expensive," Tim said. "The euro is strong; the dollar is weak. We've already overspent."

"But," I protested, "this may be the chance of a lifetime. Besides, isn't your Uncle James buried somewhere in France?"

"I'm not sure. Mom never talks about it."

I was positive he wanted to go. Tomorrow might be our only chance ever. So I pressed.

"We should do the tour, Hon, even if it means charging it on our American Express card. It's something we'll never have the opportunity to do again."

It was a lot of money in euros; I didn't even want to know the equivalent in dollars. I repeated my mantra with the clincher.

"Let's do it. When will we ever be this close again? It's my Christmas gift to you."

The wake-up call came at 5:30 AM. We sipped coffee in silence and met our guide in the lobby. By 6:15 we were winding our way northward to Normandy Beach. The biting wind had picked up as we reached La Pointe du Hoc, a monument erected halfway between Omaha and Utah beaches. I buttoned my coat, wound my scarf tightly, and wished I had worn earmuffs and boots as we emerged from the minivan.

The gun battery and concrete bunkers top the bluffs that open onto the sea, with a gray setting of sky, bunkers, and gun turrets. In 1944, the ranger objective was to scale the one-hundred-foot cliff and defeat the German army. Two hundred and twenty-five rangers accomplished the mission but amassed heavy casualties.

Omaha Beach possessed an eerie stillness, a feeling that many spirits still guarded the shoreline. Tim and I slogged through mud to the bluff's crest to view the harbor still laden with sunken vessels that provided a land bridge for the Allied forces. At the Caen Museum, an interactive media explained further World War II battles and the European campaign.

The afternoon schedule rounded out our tour with the Normandy Cemetery at St. Laurent-sur-Mer, 170 miles from Paris. While our companions visited the Memorial Gardens, Tim and I headed to the Visitors' Center. Since we were the sole visitors, Tim asked the hostess how to locate a family member buried in one of the French military cemeteries. She plugged the vital statistics into her database and summarily disappeared. Seconds later, she reappeared wearing a trench coat and carrying a tray. She asked if we would like to visit the gravesite. Stunned by her remark, Tim nodded, and I followed. Still a bit shaken, we climbed into the vinyl-swathed golf cart. Our hostess drove to Plot H, Row 11, Grave Number 19. She smoothed a clay substance over the recessed letters on the white marble cross; the name and dates popped out. She snapped several Polaroids: date of death, eleven days after D-Day. I couldn't look at Tim. My eyes were glistening. The surreal feeling of actually being at Normandy Beach and viewing the gravesite of PFC James E. Lee was penetrating me. Tim's Uncle James was someone I had heard about for more than thirty-five years, and here was his final resting place.

Our hostess gave us the option of returning to the Center or remaining at the gravesite. More emotionally overwhelmed than we had bargained for, Tim thanked her and said we'd stay. A sympathetic smile said she had seen our reactions before—finite minds struggling to grasp our discovery, drink in the reality of lives lost, and experience the tremendous grief of this place. No words came, only tears burning our cheeks. A large lump wedged itself in my throat, so I didn't speak. My heart was full for mothers like Mama Lee, who had lost a son on foreign soil, and for young, courageous soldiers like the nineteen-year-old from west Georgia who had left his home and family, including his twelve-year-old sister (now my mother-in-law), to serve his country even if it meant his life.

Uncle James rests with his comrades-in-arms under a bronze statue depicting the "Spirit of American Youth Rising from the Waves." Plot H faces the reflection pool and circular chapel. Like Pearl Harbor, this consecrated ground yields a deafening silence louder than the rushing winds and lapping waves. The chapel carillon began to play a military anthem. It was time to start back.

We took one last look at the white cross bearing James Lee's name, rank, date of birth and death, and one last photo. Tim reverently touched the marker, memorizing this moment.

"I'd give anything if Mom and Dad could see this," he said. I nodded.

The marker was one of thousands, each a simple reminder of a single life given for a cause. A glance in any direction showed row upon row of identical crosses and Jewish stars dotting the evergreen lawn—nine thousand in this cemetery alone.

I felt a rush of emotion at this realization, and I wiped my nose. We clasped hands and silently strolled among the trees bent double by the wind. A strange mingling of thankfulness and grief filled me as we returned to the minivan.

On the return trip, Tim and I didn't say anything for a while. It was one of those moments that people who have been married a long time understand. We didn't need words to express ourselves. Finally, my husband of thirty five years looked at me with shining eyes.

"It was worth it," he whispered, "every penny."

"Think not upon their passing. Remember the glory of their spirit." My thoughts exactly as we pay silent homage to the thousands of Uncle Jameses who guaranteed our freedom.

I gave my husband the Normandy trip for a Christmas gift, but I received more than I could ever give. The gift of Normandy Beach was one that I will remember the rest of my life.

Sheila S. Hudson

Caroling with the Coots

A few years ago, my husband, Bud, started a harmonica band, the Harmonicoots, for residents of Sun City—a retirement community for people fifty-five and over—in Roseville, California, where we live. Within months, the band, more than sixty men and women strong, got good enough to perform seventy gigs in public at various venues and events.

Last year, the Coots, as they are affectionately known, decided to go Christmas caroling in our community, organizing three gigs per night for three consecutive nights in December. Their aim was to go to the homes of shut-ins and disabled people, play and sing Christmas carols for about a half-hour, and then move on to the next house.

That first night, as he was getting ready to go, Bud asked me if I wanted to join them.

"I'd feel like a fifth wheel," I told him. "How on Earth can a person who doesn't play the harmonica, can't sing worth a lick, and would only be in the way, contribute to caroling?"

"Just your presence would be enough," he said.

"Yeah, right," I retorted.

I thought about it long and hard. I would love to go caroling with the Coots, but there were so many reasons to stay home. The only musical instrument I'd ever played was the guitar, which I hadn't picked up in forty years. Then there was my voice. I remember my college chorus teacher asking another singer and me not to sing, just to mouth the words during a performance. Worse, cold weather really bothers me. I shake uncontrollably, and my teeth chatter. When my ears get too cold, I get a pounding headache. If I joined the Coots for caroling, one of two things would happen: they'd suffer, or I'd suffer.

But then, I thought, *I'd miss out on all the fun and camaraderie. And where was my Christmas spirit?* The yuletide season was made for sharing and caring and bringing joy to one another, right? If I stayed home, I'd be another Scrooge, "bah-humbugging" all night. I decided to follow my heart instead of my head. I decided to go.

First, I put on Bud's long johns under my slacks, added layers of sweaters and socks, found some cashmere-lined gloves, and donned the thickest ear muffs I could find. That took care of the cold. As for my voice, I had no problem not singing. That was a blessing even to me. But how could I fully participate in a musical event with nothing to play? I resigned myself to either hiding in the background, silently observing the festivities, or waiting in the car to chauffeur a few people to the next stop. Either way, it looked like it was going to be a long night. *Oh, well,* I thought, *at least I won't freeze.*

Just as we were bundling up in coats and Santa hats, I noticed the large jingle-bell wreath I had hung on the inside our front door. At the last minute, I grabbed it and hid it in the back seat. When we got inside the first house, I pulled the wreath out from under my coat. Bud looked at me in amazement, but I shrugged and said, "I have to play something!" When some thirty Coots began to play and sing "Jingle Bells," what a difference those bells made! Everyone was smiling and looking my way, happy that I'd found a way to add to the merriment of the evening.

That magical night, at our first house, we played for an elderly couple who had been ill for months. As we spilled into their living room, I noticed the husband hooked up to an oxygen tank, while his frail wife suffered from severe arthritis. She clapped to the music with gnarled hands, while he tapped his fingers on his armchair. Later, he told us, "Thank you. This is the best Christmas we've had in years."

The second house was just as memorable. Two of the Coots, Elmer and Jeannie, professional singers in a local band, brought smiles of awe and wonder to the neighbors with their harmonized version of "Silent Night." One sweet lady, her hands leaning on a walker, was so moved by the music that she had tears streaming down her face.

Our visit to the third house brought tears to our eyes. We went to the home of Rosemary Erkel, whose daughter told us it was the first time her mother had been out of bed in a year. Her face peaceful and glowing as if from an inner fire, Rosemary, dressed in a bright red outfit and warm slippers, sat in her wheelchair in her living room as the Coots played and sang to her and her family. At times she'd sing along with us; other times she'd close her eyes to savor the moment as if it were a feast she was enjoying one bite at a time. This was her last Christmas with us— Rosemary died soon afterward.

Now, as I glance over the upcoming schedule of caroling, I can't wait to accompany the Coots again, slapping those bells against my palm to "Jingle Bells," "Deck the Halls," and other joyful songs, hoping to brighten the holidays for our neighbors and friends. I no longer worry about making a contribution. Instead, I feel gratified by the gifts I receive just by taking part. My spirit soars to the internal rhythm of love and compassion, which reaches out to all those lonely souls whose homes we visit. My heart sings, even though my voice can't. Best of all, remembering the childlike delight on all those radiant faces keeps me warm the whole year long. Caroling with the Coots, once a dreaded event, has become my favorite Christmas gift to myself.

Jennifer Martin

Cass Park Church's carolers were always
ready to make necessary adjustments.

Bearing Gifts

*The greatest good you can do for
another is not just share your riches,
but to reveal to him his own.*

Benjamin Disraeli

Christmas with my brother, Ken, was always a magical time. He never got "too cool" for excitement over the holidays the way the rest of us did. Ken was born smack in the middle of my parents' twelve kids. He was born a month early in an era when pediatric intensive care units weren't what they are today. Halfway through the delivery, the doctors realized the umbilical cord was wrapped around Ken's throat, cutting off the oxygen to his brain. By the time he was in the doctor's arms, it had been cut off long enough to leave him with cerebral palsy, mild retardation, and profound deafness. But God is good, and he more than compensated for Ken's handicaps by lavishing on him a sparkling personality, a zest for life, and a childlike faith that worked like a magnet to attract everyone around him.

Because my brother, Mark, was born less than a year after Ken, and my sister, Gail, had been born ten months earlier, babying Ken was not an option. He was part of the gang from day one, and although he didn't walk until he was twelve, he never had trouble keeping up with the rest of us, or the passel of neighborhood kids and cousins who hung around our house.

In the hospital, the doctors had advised my parents not to even see Ken, to place him in a special home and forget they'd had him. They predicted he'd never walk or talk, never feed himself, and wouldn't live past his tenth birthday. Ken was seven by the time I was born, and I'm glad the doctors never told him any of that. The Ken I knew was lean and taut, feisty and impish, and ate anything that didn't eat him first. He loved a party, loved being the center of attention, and loved everything to do with Christmas.

One of my favorite Christmas memories was a year when our grandparents sent us a new swing set. From first glance, Ken was fascinated with the slide. He spent the holidays on the ground offering a blow-by-blow commentary as the rest of us slid down. He'd squeal with delight as we began to slide, throw his head back and laugh when we landed with a splat at his feet, then chase us on all fours, trying to grab us and tickle us before we could crawl back up the ladder and out of reach. He never tried to traverse the ladder himself, though. His scrawny, twisted legs just didn't work that way.

The day the rest of us started back to school, Mama knew what she had to do. She bundled up Ken, took him out to the backyard, pointed him toward the ladder, and began to pray. "Okay, Lord, Ken wants to go down the slide. I'm gonna need all the help I can get to let him try." Years later, she told me how hard it was watching him climb and fall, climb and fall, again and again. He tore both knees out of his pants, cut one elbow, and bloodied his forehead. One particularly bad tumble left him rocking on the lawn, crying and holding a knot on the back of his head.

The neighbor to the back of us came to the fence and yelled at my mama, "What kind of woman are you? Get that baby off that ladder!" Mama told her as nicely as she could that, if it bothered her, she'd have to close her curtains and stop watching. Ken had decided he was going down the slide, and down the slide he would go, no matter how long it took him.

By the time the rest of us got home from school, Ken was black and blue, but smiling from ear to ear. Not only could he get up and down the slide with lightning speed, but heaven help the kid who got in his way.

That was a generous gift my grandparents sent us that year. I'm sure it set them back a bit. But the real gift came from my mom, my mom who loved my brother enough to watch him struggle, and to pray for the courage not to interfere, knowing how important it was for Ken to do things on his own.

That was almost fifty years ago. I wish I knew where those doctors are now. They were so ready to tell us all my brother would never do. Obviously, they didn't know the God we knew. What would they say if they could see Ken now at age fifty-five, living independently and holding down a job? They didn't know back then that God had a much bigger plan for my brother, and they didn't know the mama who loved him enough and trusted God enough to give him the best Christmas present he'd ever receive.

Mimi Greenwood Knight

5

CHRISTMAS TRADITIONS

Heap on the wood!
The wind is chill;
But let it whistle as it will.
We'll keep our Christmas merry still.

Sir Walter Scott

Holiday Tale

*Even as an adult, I find it
difficult to sleep on Christmas Eve.
Yuletide excitement is a potent caffeine,
no matter your age.*

Carrie Latet

Like many other people, this time of year is my favorite. People really get into the true reason for the holidays: miracles, good cheer, helping your fellow man. However, others, like me as a seven-year-old boy, only thought of one thing: presents!

Every year the holidays would come, and while my friends had millions of gifts under their trees (and in their living room for my Jewish friends), I would only get one gift. My parents would always say that we could not afford anything else. Besides, that was not the true meaning for the holidays! (As a child, I got sick and tired of that excuse.)

One year when I was eleven, I was more happy and excited than usual during the holidays. Was it because there was world peace? No. Was it because there was less hunger in Africa? No. Or even perhaps there was a cure for a terrible disease? Not even that. It was because I saw *two* gifts for me! What in the world could they be? Sure, I had been extra good during the year, but what in the world did I do to deserve *two* gifts? I really did not care. I was just so excited not to have only one gift that year.

My parents, as well as my other siblings, had gathered together. After we'd said some prayers and sung some songs, we were going to open the gifts. Anticipation was getting to me. My heart was racing. Finally, I was allowed to rip through the first wrapped package. My joy quickly turned to depression when I realized what the first gift contained: a left sock! (I'm sure you can guess what my second present would be: the right sock.)

Years later, as I've matured, I'm not so sure if that story is true or if I've just told it so many times that I *think* it's true. It really doesn't matter. I've learned that what does matter is the holiday spirit: helping others, being appreciative, and showing kindness and love. But before I take too much time in writing about the holidays, I better make sure I get down to the department store to buy my daughter a holiday present: a pair of socks. One can never forget a great ritual!

Michael Segal

The World's Biggest Table

Christmas is sights, especially
the sights of Christmas reflected in
the eyes of a child.

William Saroyan

It was the biggest table in the world, and it was filled with brightly wrapped Christmas presents. The gifts were piled so high they formed a peak in the middle of the table. This was truly a miracle to the eyes of a child. *How did they get there? Who were they for? Was it possible that one or maybe two were for me?*

This was the Christmas Eve tradition in the basement of my maternal grandparents' home for as long as I could remember. Though it is now over fifty years since my childhood, the memories are vivid and endearing.

My grandparents' home was the family meeting place for Sunday dinners and all holidays, birthdays, anniversaries, christenings, weddings, funerals—you get the picture. Grandma cooked, and her five sons, two daughters, their families, and extended families ate. Christmas Eve was the culmination of the year's feasts.

Though my grandparents' home was large, all meal preparation, eating, and socializing took place in the basement. There was a full kitchen, bathroom, small seating area, and the biggest table in the world. Now, remember, my memory of this table is from the perspective of a very young child. However, as I look back, it had to be a very big table to seat the number of people in the family.

The furnace was in the middle of the basement. In a vain attempt to hide the furnace, my grandmother had placed her curtain stretcher in front of the furnace. The curtain stretcher always had a lace curtain stretched from end to end that was held to the easel by small nails around the frame.

Family and friends began arriving early on Christmas Eve. The adults drank homemade red wine (prepared by enterprising neighbors) and exchanged stories. They toasted to each other's good health and wished each other well.

The children (siblings and cousins) grouped together on the far side of the basement, trying to figure out where the presents were and what they would receive. We played games, ate, and ran around the basement. Our parents, aunts, uncles, and grandparents ignored us, knowing there was no place for us to go, or to get into trouble, for we were rarely out of their sight.

Grandma called us to the table, and Christmas Eve dinner began with a hearty antipasto. Platters filled with roasted peppers, hot peppers, fragrant cheeses, lettuce, and artichoke hearts were passed. The passed platters were followed quickly with baskets of hot Italian bread and homemade bread sticks.

The antipasto was cleared from the table, and the pasta was next. Grandma preferred regular spaghetti—nothing fancy like linguine, fusilli, or ziti. She thought thin spaghetti wasn't "real," so we feasted on regular spaghetti topped with a delicious marinara sauce and lots of parmesan cheese.

Throughout the dining experience, conversation continued, and with the addition of more wine, our voices grew louder. The children sat at the end of the table on benches brought in from the outdoor picnic table. We were seated closely to make maximum use of the benches. Since we weren't trusted to pass the heavy platters, our dishes were prepared by nearby adults.

Fried fish and steamed shrimp filled the next course, accompanied by fresh vegetables cooked to perfection. More bread, more wine, more conversation . . . what fun and noise! Hours passed, and it was time for dessert.

The children were given ice cream in cups, topped with whipped cream and a cherry. The adults enjoyed espresso coffee with plates of fresh fruit and cheese. Soon, plates of Italian pastries filled the table—cannoli, napoleons, rum cakes, and cookies topped with pignoli nuts. Diet? What is a diet?

The children soon tired of sitting and were excused from the table. The women cleared and washed the dishes, while the men began loading the table with gifts that appeared mysteriously. Since the children were busy in another part of the basement, they were not paying attention to the ever-growing gift table. "Children, close your eyes," one of the adults would announce. We stopped playing and quickly closed our eyes.

"We will come and get you, but you must keep your eyes closed. Okay?"

"Yes, yes, our eyes are closed. We are ready!" we shouted in unison.

As we were led to the table, the overhead lights were turned out. As we opened our eyes, the lights went on, and there was the treasure. The biggest table in the world no longer held food, but instead gifts piled high to the ceiling. What wonder! What more could any child want? This was truly a dream come true.

And then it began. Gifts were passed out by one adult after another to each other and to the children. Most presents were real, but some adult gifts were gags—fun packages presented from brother to brother or sister to sister-in-law containing an item that represented a private joke or an inappropriate style, size, or color. Everyone laughed and eagerly awaited the next presentation.

Hours passed, and the table was still piled with gifts. "Let's take a break," said one of the aunts, "and sing some carols!" The basement filled with the glorious sounds of family singing. Even if you did not know the words, you hummed along just to be a part of the fun.

We began opening the gifts again. As we received a special toy or game, we wanted to play. We would back away from the table and sit on the floor to see how our toy worked or our doll cried. Some of the smaller children began to fall asleep. Grandma would put two or three chairs together, place a blanket and pillow on the hard surface, and create a makeshift bed in the middle of all the chaos.

Soon, the last few gifts remained, and one of the uncles would announce, "We always save the best for last and the best for the best! The best wife, mother, mother-in-law, and grandmother in the world now gets her presents."

Until that moment, I did not realize Grandma had not received any of the presents. She received her gifts at the end of the evening. That was also a tradition—a tradition that was kept until her last Christmas Eve.

The biggest table in the world was now empty—no food, no gifts, nothing on the table. The tablecloth was removed for cleaning and ready for the next day's meal. Some of us went home; others stayed at our grandparents' home for the night. All of us returned the next day for Christmas dinner.

Many years later, when my grandparents had passed away and their home was torn down to make way for a newer home, I wondered what ever happened to that table. No one seemed to know for sure. It didn't matter. I knew where it was. The biggest table in the world lived in my memory forever.

Helen Xenakis

All I Want for Christmas

I am on the phone with my daughter, Margot, who lives in San Francisco. We are embroiled in our annual Christmas conversation.

"I'm cutting back this year."

"Mom, you say that every year. I'm thirty seven years old. Just do it. I can cope. So, what do you want for Christmas?" Margot asks.

What I don't want is another large book. My coffee table runneth over. And, please, no high-tech gifts. Three years' worth of pictures languish in my digital camera, never to see an album. And don't even think about an iPod. I have no idea how all those songs find their way into that tiny container. I have three remotes for the TV, VCR, and DVD player. I'm sure one of them records stuff, but I haven't a clue which one. The remote governing the stereo is lost. Good riddance. And messages pop up on my computer screen warning me that my memory is low. What am I to do? I'm from the on-off generation. I don't need any more buttons to push.

You ask me what I want. I want you to come home. I want to wake up on Christmas morning and watch my grandchildren tear through bright wrapping paper. I want to hear your laughter from the kitchen as you and your siblings prepare breakfast, like you did many Christmases ago. I want to cook you roast beef, pour you red wine, and see your face in the candlelight. And I want you at the table when we all join hands as we thank God for this food and each other.

"Mom, did you hear me? What do you want for Christmas?" Margot's voice pokes through my musings.

"Oh, a cookbook would be nice. Or maybe an apron."

Alice Malloy

Milestones in the Boughs

Yesterday is history.
Tomorrow is a mystery. And today?
Today is a gift. That's why we call it a present.

Babatunde Olatunji

I've taken a few days off work to ready my home for Christmas. The only thing left is decorating the tree, and I've saved that for last. While a pot of coffee brews, I turn on my favorite carols, build a small fire in the fireplace, then place boxes of ornaments on the couch.

Most of my ornaments are old. Some were painstakingly created by hand. Some were gifts from friends and family. Others, I bought on a whim. But my dearest ornaments, by far, are the dated ones.

I married in 1980 and couldn't wait for Christmas. I wanted to buy one of those ornaments that said, "Our First Christmas Together," a romantic and perfect touch.

While shopping one evening, I found it—a young couple snuggled together in a sleigh, while a black stallion pulled them through the snow. Across the bottom it read, "Our First Christmas Together," and was dated 1980. I carried the glass ball home, carefully hung it on the tree, and a tradition was born.

Every holiday since, I've purchased a Christmas ornament that symbolizes an event or milestone during the year. It's always something we can look at and easily say, "Yeah, that was the year we. . . ." Sometimes the ideal ornament isn't dated, so I mark the year on it myself.

The routine for hanging them remains the same. I start with the oldest and work up. I've repeated this ritual since 1980 and still enjoy the familiar rhythm of placing each ornament on the tree. They represent the years of my life.

Let's be clear. Some years are quite unbearable. They present challenges that try our very souls and rip our hearts apart. Like 1982, when I had my first surgery and heard doctors say that conceiving a child was unlikely. But here's the dated ornament from 1982, bearing the image of a young girl in a blue dress. To me, it signified hope.

Four years later, with our hopes fading, my husband and I received an opportunity to adopt. We knew it was a miracle, and when the doctor called and said, "You've got a girl!" I cried tears of joy and thanksgiving, as I do every year when I uncover a small heart-shaped ornament, with a rocking horse and the words, "Baby's 1st Christmas 1986," embroidered on it.

The following year found us between houses, living in a cramped upstairs apartment with no windows. I purchased fabric, trim, and patterns, and made dozens of ornaments while living there, all in an attempt to stay sane.

But thank God for fun years like 1994. We bought a used camper and vacationed in the Smoky Mountains. How fitting to discover a Christmas ornament shaped like a tent and titled "Campin' Companions."

Sometimes I find ornaments in unlikely places. When my dear mother-in-law died, I saved a tiny brass music note from a funeral floral arrangement and penned the year on it. She was an accomplished musician, and it's a perfect reminder of her life.

There was our first SUV, a visit to The White House, a trip to New Orleans, the loss of our beloved collie, our daughter's graduation, and the horrifying events of 9/11.

Now, as evening shadows gather at the windows, one ornament remains—an elegant porcelain heart, marking twenty-five years of marriage.

Steadying it on the tree for the first time, I am filled with a host of emotions. I know what it took to get here. The joy and the pain, the laughter and the tears, the memories and milestones—it's all on the tree.

My ornament collection affirms that life is full of seasons. People die; babies are born. Just as hope fades, miracles happen. Not every year is a good one, but no matter what the year brings, if I look carefully, there's always something good to remember.

Dayle Allen Shockley

"You can hardly see the tree. Next year, why
don't we just make one big pile of ornaments!"

Taking Down the Christmas Tree

The house is now quiet. The process of taking down the festive decorations, and especially the Christmas tree, always brings a wave of sadness. It marks the end of a point in my life that cannot be experienced again. A flood of memories comes rushing back, and I savor those times when my children and I experienced such joyous times. As I take down each ornament and lay it away for another year, I remember the significance of each one. There's the little brown lion my son made for me in the third grade. Over the years, it lost one leg, but it still hangs proudly on the tree year after year. I remember the ornaments my daughter made by hand for me when she attended college and didn't have enough money to buy a present. Sometimes, those presents are the most cherished.

I remember the good times. I remember the lean times when there wasn't enough money to buy a tree on which to hang the ornaments. Somehow, things always turned out all right. I remember when the children were young and so excited to hang the ornaments on the tree. But I also remember the teen years when they could have cared less.

Life is made up of memories, and as I once again take down the Christmas decorations, I have yet another Christmas to put into my very special memory bank.

Dr. Lyla Berry

Christmas Found

*Christmas is most truly Christmas
when we celebrate it by giving the light of
love to those who need it most.*

Ruth Carter Stapleton

Preparing amid the hustle and bustle for the upcoming Christmas season was truly maddening. Schedules to meet and deadlines to attend were pounding at the doorstep. A whirlwind of anxious forgetfulness flooded down like endless packages frantically begging to be wrapped. The stores were jam-packed with people of all kind. Grocery stores, clothing stores, bookstores—it didn't matter—the buzz of the season was in the air, in symphony with souls "on edge." The freeways, highways, main roads, and back roads seemed to fill as quickly as the opening of Disneyland's theme park. *Where was everyone off to?* one would wonder. This was supposedly the season of giving and loving, one to another—when hearts emerged a little lighter with joy and arms opened with giving affection. At what point did all the magic cease? What happened to the enchantment of Christmas? Perhaps it was tucked away back in the days of childhood, never to be regained. Something needed to change—but what?

Suddenly, a request from the local radio station playing in the background caught my attention. "This year, they're forecasting a record for cold temperatures. The local homeless shelter is in desperate need of clothing— hats, scarves, and gloves especially. A three-day window has been set up to receive donations into the late hours of the night." Something pulled at my heartstrings that very moment—a tinge of a feeling almost forgotten. *This is the answer!* I immediately thought. Then, as if flying on wings, I packed up my three-year-old son and headed out to the local discount store.

The crowds in the store didn't budge my determination. Four sets of hats, gloves, and scarves were found within a matter of minutes and purchased before I even knew it. Four small brown paper bags were also bought, each with an orange inside and a copy of an unforgettable story of some orphan boys who received only one Christmas gift—an orange. *How fitting,* I suddenly realized. We were on our way.

Back in the car, the same radio station was playing holiday music, but this time it seemed to capture my senses. The previous announcement came on again, asking for donations and stating newfound information:

"The number of homeless men sleeping outside in the brisk icy cold reached a record of 200 last night. The shelter is packed to the walls, exceeding its maximum occupancy with women and children. Still more at the door need to come in."

My attention was again brought to the present as my patient three-year-old son finally asked where we were going. I explained that certain people needed warm gloves, hats, and scarves. They didn't live in a house of their own and needed us to help. His face held a look of puzzlement. How does one explain such a thing to a three-year-old? Restlessness got the better of him as he pleaded with me to go to the candy store instead. He carefully retrieved from his pocket his very first dollar bill. It had been given to him a few days earlier—a possession so precious that if anyone even looked at it, he immediately retreated out of sight with the dollar in hand. It had become his priceless treasure. I promised his pleading eyes that we would definitely go to the candy store after we dropped off the bags. Though he whined a little, he seemed okay with it, as long as we hurried.

At last, we reached the entrance to the drop-off center. The scene before me took my breath away while jump-starting my dormant heart. A line had formed with about five cars in front of me and more coming in behind me. Trunkloads of bags were being retrieved and put into an enormous truck for the shelter. Nearing our stop, I noticed countless men and women staggering along the sidewalk. A woman was crying with joy—hand to mouth—vocalizing again and again her disbelief at what was happening before her. I, too, felt the awe of what was transpiring. Within the slums of the city, hearts of goodness were answering to a call in need.

We finally reached the head of the line. I helped my son out of the car and handed him one of the bags. He was a little hesitant and questioned the surroundings. I could see his eyes taking in everything, yet somehow knowing that he was helping these people in need. The worker's broad smile lit up his face as he bent down and slowly took the gift from my son. He thanked us repeatedly and assured us many times how ever so grateful someone would be for these little bundles.

With a wish of "Merry Christmas," I turned to go back to the car, reaching for my son's hand. He looked up at me with the most solemn brown eyes as he simply said,

"Wait." Digging into his pocket with his sweet, little dimpled hands, he retrieved his dollar—his most beloved treasure—and very slowly gave it to the worker, wishing him "Merry Christmas." The man tenderly took it, somehow sensing that my son was giving everything he had ever possessed in his innocent little world. The worker again repeated over and over his grateful thanks, telling him that it would be put to use for something very special. I was completely stunned, looking into this little face of beaming innocence. He knew he had done something extraordinary, and that same feeling magically found its way to me. This innocent act of charitable kindness far surpassed anything I had ever witnessed. Among all the annoying chaos of the city—the hustle and bustle of the season—the true meaning of the season was found! I had found what was once lost, dwelling within the heart of a child.

I gathered this little person in my arms as my tears welled up, nestled him close, and whispered, "Thank you." A day that had started out in frazzled chaos had evolved into an unexpected moment of awakening joy and contentment.

This scene has since become a favorite family tradition, one that rescues the heart and soul in the knick of time during the chaos of the season—a priceless gift for the giver and recipient alike.

Lisa May

Christmas Cards

Let's face it: it's that time of year again. And I don't just mean it's time to trim trees or hang lights or buy gifts. I mean it's time to get out the gold pen and the holiday stamps, and send out the annual Christmas cards!

Make no mistake about it, choosing the right card takes a lot of thought. Are you the type who likes cuddly baby animals or more of a religious theme? Do you prefer reindeer, Santa Claus, or winter snow scenes? Or are you, like my friend Shirley, more of the gingerbread man type?

So this year I've decided to bypass the whole card-choosing issue and do what any typical, proud mother would do: find a picture of my family and turn it into a card.

I started by sorting through the past year's batch of pictures for one where my entire family looked happy, relaxed, and well-tanned, preferably taken somewhere in nature. Not too much to ask, right? But, shockingly enough, after going through several stacks, I found, you guessed it, not one single picture that fit this criteria. So I went back through and tried to find a picture with three of us smiling and one of us with good hair. Then I tried to find a picture with most of us clean and sort of grimacing. And then finally just any picture that had all four of us in it fully dressed at the same time. Still nothing, except for one taken in the midnineties on the day we brought my son home from the hospital. But this would only shock and confuse people.

It was obvious from all this that we needed to get a new picture taken just for the card. So we all got into our good velvet clothes, and I called my neighbor Linda to come over with her camera.

"Quick, come and take our picture," I hissed into the phone, "before someone gets a runny nose or sneezes or picks up the cat or something."

Now Linda is an avid picture taker, so you'd think that chances are that least one picture would come out decent enough to use as a Christmas card. So imagine my surprise when I got the pictures back from being developed and saw twenty-four pictures of a rather surprised–looking, red-eyed family standing in front of various household appliances.

So I took the matter into my own hands and moved on to plan B: take pictures of the kids outside among all of the festive holiday decorations. Mind you, I use the term "festive" loosely since all we had in front of our house was a string of colored light bulbs put up sometime in 1992.

Then I remembered the upscale neighborhood three blocks away, where everyone went overboard each year with decorating their front lawn.

It was a brilliant plan.

"You can't take pictures of our children in front of strangers' houses," my husband said. "What will our friends think?"

"That we got a bigger house and trendier Christmas lights?"

"Very funny."

The good news is that these pictures came out great. I took fabulous shots of my children posing in front of cutout wooden snowmen, reindeer, and even between the three wise men in a miniature cardboard manger.

The bad news is that in the end my husband was right. It just seemed, well, deceitful to send them out. Instead, I chose a rather plain picture of the kids sitting on the living-room floor holding an ornament.

But that's okay. You see, today I received a photo Christmas card from my old college friend Lisa who lives in a condo in south Florida. It was a lovely scene of her family gathered around a cozy fireplace mantel holding a cat. As far as I know, she doesn't own a cat or, for that matter, a fireplace. In fact, now that I take a closer look, I'm not even sure that's her real husband!

But, somehow, that comforts me.

Debbie Farmer

Paper Chains

Pleasure is spread through the earth in stray
gifts to be claimed by whoever shall find.

William Wordsworth

Christmas is coming. I know this like I know my age, weight, and password to my Yahoo account. Lest I forget this fact, I have my own useful visual tracker hanging from the baker's rack. This ticker is made of red and green construction paper links stapled together in a simple AB pattern. We call it: The Chain.

I can't remember the year my sister-in-law, Christi, and I came up with The Chain. It must have been when we were idealistic twenty-somethings, and visions of cherry-cheeked, pajama-clad children icing unburnt sugar cookies danced in our heads.

Kylie was two-and-a-half when she stayed with me while Christi and Rudy traveled to Germany for a wedding. She did not understand the slow passing of days without her mother, but she understood "nighty-night." I made a countdown chain of paper moons. Every night, she'd tear off one yellow link. She could see how many more nights until Mama would snuggle her to sleep again. It turned out to be an ideal representation of elapsing time, easy for young minds as well as hands to grasp. Sometime after the trip to Germany, and before the children grew mustaches, we decided to make a countdown chain for Christmas.

This sounds simple. It shouldn't be much trouble to make twenty-five one-by-nine-inch strips and staple them together, right? (I prefer stapling over gluing—who has time to hold and count to one thousand ten before moving on?) If we had known this tradition would take hold with the consistency of figgy pudding, we might have rethought our grand chain. But it is not just a countdown chain; it is a countdown *activity* chain. Change those first two letters around, lose a "ti," and you have "cavities." Stay with me here. I'm about to make a connection. December is full enough of sweets and treats and time demands. We've created a decadent activity countdown chain that challenges the minty freshness of anyone's goodwill. What's to blame here? Is it motherhood, teacherhood, or the constant lure of insanity?

Come Thanksgiving, the kids are already bugging us. "When are you making The Chain? Can we make The Chain today? Mom, Mom, Mom, chain, chain, chain. Mom, chain, all the way." It starts to sound like an old prison chant—to the tune of "Jingle Bells." And so the planning begins.

Christi prints out two December calendars. Each of us writes down all the things already on our calendar, like gymnastics, school concerts, holiday programs, and church events. Then we brainstorm a list of additional activities that we think the kids would like to do. We plan simple things for already packed school nights, like delivering a poinsettia to someone special, drinking hot cocoa with a candy-cane stir stick, or finding a wrapped gift on the movie shelf (open and enjoy). On weekends, we schedule more time-consuming activities, like cleaning our rooms for Santa, making rice crispy treats with home-made marshmallows, or chopping a cord of wood for the neighbor.

That's when the coordination happens. We plan the entire month of December, synchronizing days and events like the goddesses we are. Unfortunately, things don't always work out as planned. Take day five: Make a garland out of starlight mints. First, I had to make a special trip for starlight mints. The three bags I bought had candies in sleeves, without twisted ends of cellophane. Who on earth can tie those tiny wings together? Not possible. So, my nine-year-old daughter, Emily, and I spent a few hours wrapping starlight mints in green plastic wrap and tying curly ribbon between the candies. I thought of Christi at her place doing the same things with her kids and wondered how her garland was going. I later heard that it didn't take her long to get out the old, crusty glue gun and start hot-gluing her mints together. Too bad my stapler didn't go through hard candy.

To complicate traditions, I have a fourteen-year-old this Christmas. His passion for The Chain has, shall we say, dimmed, if not lost its luster altogether. He informed me several times that he didn't think we should do The Chain this year, that the activities were, in a word, silly. My heart sank a little as I agreed that he may feel too old to participate in The Chain any longer, and I'd respect his feelings. "But remember, son, Emily is only nine, so let's not squelch her enthusiasm." He opted out of most of the activities, but that's not to say he's not involved in Christmas; he's just traded tasks. Instead of making gar-land, he stood on the roof (to my stomach-quivering hor-ror) and put up the outside lights. He passed on riding the Santa Train but dragged a large, heavy pinion pine a half-mile over the sagebrush hills of Brunswick Canyon. He didn't decorate the tree, but he got it in the stand. I couldn't have thought up all the new things he's doing this year—this man-boy who stands taller than me, talks deeply, and wears a shadow on his upper lip.

The Chain is a countdown to Christmas—a visual representation and a chance to make the most of the gifts this season has to offer. It's become a tradition laden with memories of decorating gingerbread houses, donating gifts to others, and caroling on cold December nights. It's a reminder that the journey is more important than the destination, that every day counts. I can look in Emily's cornflower blue eyes and pause without watching milliseconds fly by. I can savor a smile from Andrew in all his teenage glory and hold it close to my heart. And maybe this tradition is a mother's way to slow down the invisible ticker inside us, the one that says our kids are growing up, and someday won't be children anymore. Just maybe, if we do it half-right, those links we form with them will be stronger than paper, softer than steel, and easily reparable with a little hot cocoa and a candy-cane stir stick.

Thirteen days to Christmas. Who wants to make an origami donkey?

Tracy Schmid

The Christmas Bagel

. . . And with its shining radiance light,
Our tree of faith on Christmas night.

Thelma J. Lund

The first time I celebrated Christmas, I was twenty-nine. That's the year I met my husband, Mark, and traveled to Maryland to visit his family for the holidays.

I'm Jewish, but I thought I understood Christmas. I had visited Rockefeller Center many times to see the Christmas tree, watched the skaters laughing and slipping on the ice below, smelled chestnuts roasting, or listened to jangling bells on horse-drawn buggies in Central Park. And who could miss Santa at Macy's, the stores brimming over with toys, and carolers singing holiday cheer? When I was growing up, Christmas filled our neighborhood. Christmas day, the kids came out with enormous grins, boasting about new skates, bikes, and Monopoly sets.

Nevertheless, I didn't really understand Christmas until that year with Mark's family. His siblings traveled from east and west for a heart-warming tradition that whittled away the year's separation. I marveled at the tree brushing the ceiling with homemade ornaments, stockings hanging over a roaring fire, and green and red sugar cookies disappearing in the twinkling of an eye. Like a kid in a candy shop, I sniffed the balsam-scented air, sipped eggnog with cinnamon and nutmeg, laughed at family stories I've since heard a hundred times, and watched the family open presents all wrapped in pretty bows. Christmas filled the house with so much joy that I felt I discovered a special new world, but I still maintained my Jewish heritage with resolve. After all, I had Hanukkah with dreidels, menorahs, gold coins, potato latkes, and, best of all, my family.

That second year, Mark and I celebrated Christmas in his tiny studio in Brooklyn Heights. We bought a tabletop Christmas tree. What else would fit in an apartment the size of a postage stamp? After setting it up, we left in search of our first decorations.

"Unbelievable," I said, spying an ornament in a local card shop. "It's a little transparent bulb with a plastic bagel inside suspended on a little red bow!"

Mark laughed. "Perfect. We'll put it on the tree."

"On the top," I exclaimed. "Instead of a star, it will represent the merging of our lives."

"Sure," Mark muttered. "Whatever you say, dear."

Amazing how he knew just the right words, and we weren't even married yet.

That bagel adorned the top of our little tree and continued to do so throughout the years of our engagement, marriage, and the birth of our two wonderful children, Sara and Natalie.

In fact, our children, who celebrate both Christian and Jewish holidays, accepted that ornament as naturally as a cat drinks milk. They didn't know any better—until one day when Sara came home from school in December with a class assignment.

"We have to bring in a holiday memento that's special to our family," she said with a worried look on her face. "And tell why it's special. What should I bring?"

"Why, the bagel ornament, of course," I said, without hesitation. "It's been in our family for over ten years."

"Are you sure?" she asked. "What should I say about it?"

"You can describe how Mommy is Jewish and Daddy is Christian, and how it's a symbol of how we celebrate and honor our differences."

"Say that again," she said.

Together we wrote it down and practiced it. I was overjoyed to share our family's diversity with her second-grade class. No one, I was sure, possessed a memento quite as unique as ours. I couldn't wait for Sara to return home.

She did—crying.

"Mommy, how could you?" she sputtered with tears and a runny nose. "I was so embarrassed."

"Why?" I asked.

"Because people put stars and angels on top of a Christmas tree. Not bagels!" she said.

"But that's what makes our tree special."

"But I don't want to be special. I just want to be normal like everybody else!"

"Oh, honey," I said, "when you're older, you'll understand. From now on, we'll keep our bagel ornament our own little secret."

"I don't want it," she said. "I want a star on top of the tree!"

"Okay, we'll put a star on top. And we'll put the bagel somewhere else on the tree."

"No," she insisted. "No bagel."

That was going too far. Eventually, we compromised. We hid the bagel behind some thick needles and then covered it with garland and a colored ball. It was barely visible.

Since then, we've added ornaments to our growing collection, and every year, I ask the same question.

"Where shall we put the bagel?"

At first, it moved from its hiding place to a visible spot at the bottom of the tree. Eventually, it inched its way up branch by branch. Until one year, Sara allowed me to place it just below the star at the top.

Then, things changed drastically. Sara and Natalie decided they wanted to decorate the tree by themselves, no adults needed. They were teenagers and had to prove their independence.

I left them alone with hooks and boxes of ornaments and then crept out of the room with a bittersweet mix of emotions. My grown-up girls didn't need me anymore, but they'd learned to love and treasure our family traditions. In fact, they'd spent their own money to buy gifts for family and friends, wrapped them without help, and placed them under the tree with pride.

Despite numerous attempts to pass through the family room on the pretense of some important errand, my daughters confined me to the kitchen until they were done. When I was allowed back in, the eight-foot tree sparkled with festive lights, garland, colored balls, and a hundred family ornaments.

And there, on the very top of the tree, sat the little plastic bagel in its cracked transparent ball, suspended by its tattered red ribbon.

"How do you like the tree?" they asked, with smiles lighting up their faces.

I answered them silently as a tear rolled down my cheek.

Barbara Puccia

"I'm buying my mom something special for Christmas with my own money. Three gumball machine charms! Pretty good, huh?"

6

SPECIAL
MEMORIES

*In every conceivable manner, the family
is link to our past, bridge to our future.*

Alex Haley

A Holiday to Remember

There is no ideal Christmas;
only the Christmas you decide to make
as a reflection of your values, desires,
affections, traditions.

Bill McKibben

It was Christmas 1991, and I was worried about the impact the holidays would have on my parents. The year had been very tough on them, beginning with an accident that required both to have surgery and ending with their home burning on November 5. The Thanksgiving holiday was hard on everyone, and I was doing my part to plan a special Christmas gathering filled with happiness instead of sorrow.

My sister, Diane, and I planned every moment as if it was the first time we spent the holidays together. The dinner would be prepared by us to give my mom a break from the turmoil. She and my father had been placed in temporary housing while their home was being rebuilt. Personal items were few and far between, so any effort to prepare a meal would have been a difficult task.

Since the tree my mom had used at Christmas was destroyed in the fire, I made arrangements to purchase a smaller tabletop version. I brought it to the house and decorated it with lights and ornaments. A small star was placed on top by the grandchildren, just as was done on the larger Christmas tree each Christmas Eve. The tree soon became the centerpiece as the packages surrounded its base and ribbons sparkled with the reflections from the lights.

The small home my parents occupied soon filled with laughter as everyone arrived. The dinner was placed on the table, and we gathered together to say thanks for all we had shared the past year. We rejoiced at our triumphs and shed a tear or two over the challenges that life lay in our path, but we were thankful that it wasn't worse and felt blessed to be together for another Christmas.

After we ate, it was time to open the presents. This was the favorite part for the children. The smiles on their faces grew large, and their eyes opened wider at each gift that was passed toward their direction. They wasted no time tearing into the huge bows placed on top to see what surprise was underneath. Everyone seemed pleased with their gifts and was busy sharing with each other.

My mother disappeared from the room and came back with two smaller boxes wrapped in identical paper. Attached to each package was a card addressed to the recipient. One package was for me, and the other belonged to my sister. We were told to read the card first, so we carefully opened it to reveal the message inside:

"We wanted to give you something special this year. With money being a problem, we took our wedding rings and had them melted down to make these. The stones in each came from my engagement ring and the gold from both wedding bands. May the love bonded in these rings be passed on to you and your future generations. Mom and Dad."

Inside the packages were the most beautiful identical rings we had ever seen. I felt numb as I looked into the loving eyes of my parents sitting beside me. Although they were given tough obstacles to overcome, my parents wanted to give something special and filled with love to their children. Nothing could have been more perfect!

I still feel special whenever I think of that Christmas and the tradition it created. I have the ring they gave me, and someday I will pass it on to my daughter along with the story behind the precious gift. I want her to share with me the feeling of receiving a special gift of cherished memories.

Denise Peebles

Ringing the Doorbells of Christmas

To many people, holidays are not voyages of discovery, but a ritual of reassurance.

Philip Andrew Adams

The newspaper clipping is yellowed like a parchment scroll. The treasured article is over forty years old, written by a man who lived in the small town where I grew up. In an essay published in a church bulletin, S. L. Morgan, Sr. reminisced about two young visitors:

"One of my best Christmases was 'sparked' by the visit of two tiny girls who rang my doorbell two weeks before Christmas and left a plain tiny Christmas card they had made. Actually, that 'sparked' Christmas for me. It did something deep and wonderful in me."

I was one of those little girls.

My best friend, Claudia, and I were already counting the days until Christmas, dreaming of the toys we would find under the tree on Christmas morning. We were eight years old and getting wiser. We knew Santa might not bring everything we wanted. Like our struggling parents, Santa appeared to be on a tight budget that year.

Claudia showed me a magazine ad about selling boxes of Christmas cards to win a shiny, new bicycle and other tantalizing prizes. Inspired by the printed testimonials of enterprising boys and girls who had sold thousands of cards, Claudia and I decided to make construction-paper cards and sell them to our neighbors, hoping to earn money to buy gifts and toys. We spent one Saturday morning laboring with crayons, scissors, and paste, designing the cards that promised to bring us untold riches.

But when my mother learned of our plan to sell the cards, she vetoed it, insisting that we give away the cards instead. (My genteel Southern mother must have been mortified by the prospect of her child peddling home-made Christmas cards door-to-door.) Claudia and I reluctantly agreed to honor my mother's wishes.

We spent an afternoon ringing doorbells, hand-delivering our cards to neighbors we thought might need some Christmas cheer. We rang Mr. Morgan's doorbell and, without much fanfare, handed the white-haired gentleman one of our crayoned greetings. The lines in the old man's face melted into a smile as he read the childish cursive: "Merry Christmas! We love you."

"Thank you, girls," he said. "This is the most beautiful Christmas card I've ever received."

We thought he was just being polite, that surely the store-bought cards with gold foil and glitter were prettier than ours. Not until I read his article many years later did I realize how much our small gesture of goodwill had lifted his spirits.

After our visit, Mr. Morgan wrote later, he "began to tell neighbors, grouchy or sad, 'Listen for the joy bells.'" He urged readers to "fill the mail with millions of postals with personal notes." Over the years, Mr. Morgan continued the Christmas tradition of sending annual love notes to friends and acquaintances around the world: "I'm sure I've held many friendships intact for many years mainly by tiny love notes once a year," he wrote. "Nothing in life has paid me better."

Thanks to my mother, I am reaping the dividends of an investment made so many years before. The clipping in my scrapbook reminds me of the joy I felt as Claudia and I rang doorbells on that cold afternoon. I remember the smiling faces of the people we called on and their farewells echoing like chimes on the frozen air as we left them standing in their doorways, pleased and a little bewildered.

Several years ago, I mailed a copy of Mr. Morgan's article to Claudia. I followed his example by writing a personal note on the card, telling Claudia how much her friendship meant to me as a child, and how often I recall those years with fondness and love.

The reverberations of one afternoon continue to ring true through the years like the doorbells we rang as children on that cold December day.

Beth Copeland

The Secret of Grandma's Sugar Crock

What we are is God's gift to us.
What we become is our gift to God.

Eleanor Powell

Through the years, I've discovered bits and pieces of the past that, when put all together, make up my extraordinary grandmother, Maria Carmela Curci-Dinapoli.

I knew that she moved to this country as a young immigrant from Italy and married my grandfather, Antonio Curci, in 1910. A few years later, she was widowed with three children. I had heard family stories of how Grandma struggled to find work, to pay her debts, and to keep her family together during those difficult years. In all of these stories, one fact remained prominent—Grandma's deep religious devotion guided her through each problem and task.

But it was only recently that I would discover yet another missing piece to Grandma's past that helped me know her just that much better. My memories of her begin on an Almaden ranch in the heart of California's prune country during World War II. By then, she had married her second husband, Grandpa Tony Dinapoli, and settled into rural ranch life, raising a family of seven boys and one girl. During World War II, a government-issued flag imprinted with five blue stars hung in the front-room window of my grandparents' old farmhouse. It meant that five of their sons were off fighting in the war. Without the boys to work the land, the ranch was shorthanded. Grandma and Grandpa had to work twice as hard to produce a bountiful fruit crop.

During harvest time, every member of the family pitched in to help, including grandkids like myself. Even so, it was a difficult time for Grandma. Rationing was mandatory, there was little money, and, worst of all, there was the constant worry over whether her five sons would come home safely.

The ranch was a lovely place, especially in the spring when the orchards bloomed with white plum blossoms. During the summer, while we harvested the prune crop, Grandma cooked up fine Italian lunches. We would all sit on blankets spread out on the orchard ground, enjoying not just the wonderful food but also the satisfaction of participating in such an important family effort.

To encourage the ripe fruit to fall, Grandpa used a long wooden pole with an iron hook at the top to catch a branch and shake the prunes loose from the trees. Then the rest of us would crawl along, wearing knee pads that Grandma sewed into our overalls, and gather the plums into metal buckets. We dumped the buckets of plums into long, wooden trays, where the little purple plums were soon sun-dried into rich, brown prunes.

After a long, hard day, I walked hand-in-hand with Grandpa through the orchards while he surveyed what he had accomplished that day. I'd enjoy eating fresh plums from the trees, licking the sweet stickiness from my fingertips. On each of these walks, Grandpa would stoop down

and pick up a handful of soil, letting it sift slowly and lovingly through his strong, work-calloused hands. Then,
with pride and conviction, he would invariably say, "If
you take good care of the land, the land will take good
care of you."

As dark came on the ranch, we'd all gather together on
the cool, quiet veranda on the front porch. Grandpa
would settle comfortably into his rocker, under the dim
glow of a flickering, moth-covered light bulb, and there
he'd read the latest war news in the newspaper. Grandma
sat nearby on the porch swing, swaying and saying her
perpetual rosary. The quiet squeak of Grandma's swing
and the low mumbling of her prayers could be heard long
into the night.

The stillness of the quiet ranch house painfully reflected
the absence of the five robust young men. This was the
hardest part of the day for Grandma. The silence of the
empty house was a painful reminder that her sons were
far away, fighting for their country.

On Sunday morning, after church, Grandma was back
out on the porch again, repeating her rosary before going
into the kitchen to start cooking. Then she and Grandpa
sat at the kitchen table, counting out ration slips for the
week ahead and what little cash was available to pay the
bills. Once they finished, Grandma always took a portion
of her money and put it in an old sugar crock, placing it
high on the kitchen shelf. I often asked her what the
money in the jar was for, but she would only say, "A very
special favor."

The war finally ended, and all five of Grandma's sons
came home remarkably safe and sound. After a while,
Grandma and Grandpa retired, and the family farm turned
into part of a modern expressway.

I didn't find out what the money in that old sugar crock
was for until a week or so before last Christmas. Completely

on impulse, perhaps feeling the wonder of the Christmas season and the need to connect with its spiritual significance, I stopped at a little church I just happened to be driving past. I'd never been inside before, and as I entered the church through the side door, I was stunned to come face-to-face with the most glorious stained-glass window I'd ever seen.

I stopped to examine the intricate beauty of the window more closely. The magnificent stained glass depicted the Holy Mother and child. Like an exquisite jewel, it reflected the glory of the very first Christmas. As I studied every detail of its fine workmanship, I found, to my utter amazement, a small plaque at the base of the window that read, "For a favor received—donated in 1945 by Maria Carmela Curci-Dinapoli." I couldn't believe my eyes. I was reading Grandma's very words! Every day, as Grandma said her prayers for her soldier-sons, she'd also put whatever money she could scrape together into her sacred sugar crock to pay for the window. Her quiet donation of this window was her way of saying thank you to the Holy Mother Mary for sparing the lives of her beloved five sons.

Through the generations, the family had lost track of the window's existence. Finding it now at Christmas time, more than half a century later, not only brought back a flood of precious memories, but also made me a believer in small but beautiful miracles.

Cookie Curci

"Do you gift wrap?"

The Twelve Years of Christmas

*Blessed is the season which engages the
whole world in a conspiracy of love.*

Hamilton Wright Mabi

Since he successfully grew apples, crabapples, and rasp-
berries in the back yard of his Edmonton, Alberta, home,
my grandfather, Stan Grandish, began to look for advice
on how to successfully grow a pear tree. The general con-
sensus was that the growing season in Alberta would be
too short, and for three long years it appeared the naysay-
ers would be right. Undaunted, Grandpa continued to
nurture and care for his pride and joy. In early fall of 1985,
he triumphantly "harvested" three tiny pears from the
otherwise barren tree and proudly proclaimed his experi-
ment a success!

As it often does in the prairies, winter hit hard and early
that year, so Grandpa gave his tree only a passing glance
as he returned home on December 20 with my grandmother, Mary. He thought he saw something in the tree,
but it was dark and cold, so he decided to wait until morning to check it out.

The next morning, Grandpa looked out the kitchen window and could hardly believe his eyes! There in his tree were three large pears and a bird! Hurriedly donning his winter boots and coat, he waded through the two-feet-deep snow, returning to show Mary his prizes. Each pear was handmade from cloth and had no tags or labels. The bird, clearly a partridge, had been created by a skilled craftsperson from satin. They could find no clue to their origin.

The pears and the partridge clearly paralleled the medieval Christmas carol, "The Twelve Days of Christmas," and Grandpa thought it must be a joke around his great enthusiasm over the paltry offerings of his pear tree. He and Grandma found great pleasure in sharing their humorous story with family and friends for the rest of the holiday season. Despite their best efforts, the source of the gift remained a mystery.

The following year, Grandpa was surprised to receive a package wrapped in plain brown paper, with an illegible return address. Inside were two ceramic turtledoves. Suddenly, there was a connection to the pears and partridge received last year! Rushing downstairs, they pulled the previous year's joke out of storage. The spark that danced in Grandpa's eyes as he considered this mystery was a joy for all of us to watch. There was nothing Grandpa loved more than to solve a puzzle or outwit an opponent, and he remained confident in his ability to solve this riddle.

The next year, the mystery took on an international twist. Three handcrafted satin hens arrived from Nice, France. The return address was handwritten, so Grandpa did his best to collect handwriting specimens of everyone he knew to compare. But, alas, that holiday season also passed without a solution to the mystery.

And so it continued, year after year. In 1988, four stuffed

"calling birds" arrived by parcel post. There was no return address, but the postmark indicated it had been sent from within Canada.

On Christmas Eve of 1989, my grandparents received a call from the bus depot that a package was waiting for pickup. To their great surprise, just arrived by Greyhound from Mundare, Alberta, via Glendon, Vilna, and Vegreville (to obscure the trail), were five rings of sausage, each carefully wrapped in gold foil and arranged in a picnic basket.

By now, my grandparents looked forward each year with great anticipation to see if another "Twelve Days of Christmas" gift would arrive. And they were not alone! As news of the gentle, creative prank became public, more and more media attention became centered on my grandparents. They regularly conducted television and radio interviews across Canada, and as far away as San Diego and London, England. Articles appeared regularly in local Alberta newspapers and national magazines.

The year 1990 brought more international flair. Six white satin "geese a-laying" arrived from Spielberg, Germany, each complete with egg and nest. The following year brought seven silver-plated napkin rings shaped like swans, from Cottesloe, Australia. While my grandparents had a wide circle of friends and family, they had no connection whatsoever with these foreign locations.

In 1992, my grandparents received perhaps their favorite gift of all. Courtesy of an "Old MacDonald" in Wildwood, Alberta, Canada Post delivered a very large box containing eight wooden maids milking eight plastic cows. Each maid had a tiny crank that moved her arm in a milking motion. Predictably, no "Old MacDonald" could be located in Wildwood, Alberta, by an amused Bell Canada Directory Assistance Operator.

"Nine ladies dancing" came in the form of ballerina figurines mailed from Henrietta, New York, and in 1994, ten old-fashioned wooden "lords-a-leaping" were received from Waterloo, Ontario. They actually more closely resembled traditional toy soldiers, but by pulling a string, the arms and legs would fling up and down, mimicking a leap quite effectively. The next year, "eleven pipers piping" arrived from Burgdorf, Switzerland. There were still no clues to this long-running mystery, but my grandparents were hopeful that the twelfth and final year's gift would also include a solution. Finally, the song came to an end in 1996, as twelve wax and plastic angels "drumming" arrived from New Orleans by parcel delivery. Along with this final gift was a poem:

Ho, ho, ho, Stan and Mary,
Santa Claus makes his list,
Checks it every day,
Mystery! Surprise! Laughter!
Don't give it away,
It's a secret!
What do you say?

The next year, on December 10, 1997, a card adorned with American postage stamps mysteriously arrived in their mailbox. On the card were messages and greetings from ten different people, each in their own handwriting, and each from the destination corresponding to the origin of the gifts. This was perhaps the most mysterious of all, as my grandparents did not recognize even a single name! Several reporters also examined the card and were successful in contacting some of the people, but all said they had taken an oath of silence and refused to reveal the secret.

It appeared that the mystery would remain forever unsolved.

Then, in the summer of 1999, Grandpa suffered a serious stroke, and for the next several months his health was precarious. During this time, Grandpa's weariness only seemed to brighten when the unsolved Christmas mystery was discussed. Meanwhile, the now famous eighteen-year-old pear tree began to wither and die.

By spring, Grandpa's health had improved, and he had regained enough strength to cut down his beloved old pear tree. And then, on Father's Day, he finally got his wish. His youngest brother, Marshall, and his wife, revealed that they had been the masterminds behind the long-running mystery!

They explained that it had originally started as a gentle prank about Grandpa's dubious pear-growing attempts. When they witnessed the joy that the mystery gave him, they were compelled to carry it on year after year. To do this over the years had required enormous creativity and planning, and Marshall and Twyla had enlisted the help of many others throughout the world to help them carry on their loving gift of holiday joy and mystery.

Jeff S. Hamilton

The Last Christmas

Christmas is supposed to be a time of peace and joy on Earth, a time of giving and warmth. Many of my friends and acquaintances celebrate the day, the birth of Jesus, at church, followed by a sumptuous meal and opening gifts under the Christmas tree. Still others celebrate the day by helping those who are less fortunate at various food banks, shelters, or hospitals.

I will never forget one special Christmas. I work at Memorial Hermann Hospital, primarily in the Neuro Trauma Intensive Care Unit. Being Jewish, I also worked in other units of the hospital that day so that my Christian coworkers could spend time with their families at home on Christmas.

Walking through the large hospital, I saw several sad families in the many waiting rooms that day. I could imagine them all screaming, "What kind of Christmas is this—spending it at the hospital?" However, when I knocked on room 623 (Mrs. Hunter's room on the oncology floor), I soon learned that everything is relative.

"Hi, my name is Mike Segal from Case Management. Is there anything I can do to help you? May I come in?" I asked those questions to an eighty-seven-year-old cancer

patient who, according to the chart, would soon be transferred to a hospice so she might live out the remaining
weeks of her life more peacefully.

Her daughter Mary said, "Please come in."

As I entered the room, Mrs. Hunter uttered in a soft,
hoarse voice, "I still need a straw."

Mary quickly interjected, "They delivered this Ensure
for Mom, but they did not bring a straw. We asked the
nurse for a straw a few minutes ago, but this is Christmas,
and I don't know when the nurse will bring it."

I excused myself from the room, told the nurse what I
was doing, and rushed down to the cafeteria where I
grabbed a handful of straws. Knocking on the door again,
I was greeted by Mary's huge smile as she saw what was
in my hand.

"Thank you so much. It seems so small, but for Mom
the straw is such an important thing," Mary said as she
put the straw into the Ensure that her mother quickly
began drinking. Mary then wished me a Merry Christmas.

I replied, "May you all have a very peaceful Christmas,
too. Before I go, is there anything else I can do?"

With those words, Mrs. Hunter quickly asked in a soft
voice, "Can we sing some Christmas carols?"

That question startled me as I wasn't sure if I knew the
words to any carols, but I quickly replied, "Of course. I'd
love to."

Mrs. Hunter automatically started singing "Jingle Bells,"
and I quickly joined in, followed by her daughter. Afterward, we sang two more Christmas songs.

Some Jewish people might be asking, "How can you, as
a Jew, sing Christian songs?" However, for me the answer
was crystal clear. Judaism believes in the sanctity of life.
If I could do anything to help Mrs. Hunter enjoy her last
Christmas, I was going to do it. The preservation of life
takes precedence over everything else in Judaism, and it

may be interpreted in many different ways. That day, I interpreted it as bringing a smile to the face of a dying woman.

As we concluded our songs, Mary, with tears in her eyes, said, "Thank you so much. God bless you and Merry Christmas."

"Merry Christmas to you and your family as well," I replied, feeling the true spirit of the holiday's season.

Michael Jordan Segal

Reprinted by permission of Jonny Hawkins. ©*2007 Jonny Hawkins.*

Unexpected Guests

*E*ach *day comes bearing its own gifts.*
Untie the ribbons.

Ruth Ann Schabacker

I was six thousand miles away from home on that
snowy Christmas Eve in 1981, but it felt like a million. I
didn't look forward to the holidays; it was only my second
away from the family. For that reason, my buddy Chris
and I strolled through the mountain village of Ulmen on
our way to the club at the base in search of something to
do. We were a couple of U.S. airmen assigned to a
squadron on a German Air Force base as a NATO partner-
ship. It was still the Cold War.

As we walked by a small stone house, Chris stopped
and exclaimed, "Hey, this is Reiner and Ilona's house!"

Who the heck are Reiner and Ilona? I thought. And why would
they want us dropping by unannounced on Christmas Eve?

Enthusiastically, Chris rapped on the door several
times. I stood a distance behind him. I wasn't sure
whether they'd appreciate unexpected guests. Slowly, the
door opened, and there stood a young man wearing

glasses. "Ah, Chris!" he exclaimed. "Come in!"

"Reiner, I have a friend," Chris said as he gestured back to me.

"That's okay, I'll wait for you here," I said, not wanting to impose.

"Ah, nonsense," the young man replied. "A friend of Chris is a friend to us. Come in! Come in!"

"Hello," I said as I entered. "I'm Larry."

"Hello," the young man replied. "I am Reiner." We shook hands firmly.

Reiner was a young man with a soft demeanor, wearing steel-framed glasses and a gentle face. I soon discovered he had been a member of the German Air Force for several years and was also stationed at the base.

As I reluctantly entered the house, I found it beautifully decorated for the season. In fact, the home seemed to have a yuletide scent. I said nothing, but in my heart I let out a resounding, Wow!

"Come, Ilona is in the kitchen," Reiner said as he waved us along. As we reached the dining room, the aroma was unmistakably that of someone preparing dinner.

"Ilona," Reiner called out, *"wir haben Besuch."*

From the kitchen emerged a beautiful young woman with a slender build, auburn hair, and a warm smile. "Ah, Chris! Hello!" She embraced Chris and kissed him on the cheek. Over his shoulder, she noticed me donning a nervous smile.

"Ah, hello," she said. She walked over to me, shook my hand, and asked, "What is your name?"

"Larry," I answered nervously.

"Welcome to our home," she said. "If you are a friend of Chris, you are our friend, too." I smiled. She insisted we take off our coats, sit down, and relax. She disappeared for a moment, and returned with holiday glasses and a bottle of Riesling wine, produced in the region. She filled the

glasses and handed them out. Then, Reiner raised his glass
to propose a toast: "For friendship. You are always welcome in our home."

With a raised glass, I replied, "Thank you."

"Frohe Weihnachten," Ilona added.

"Merry Christmas," I replied, signaling I understood.

"Prost!" Reiner exclaimed, the German equivalent for
"Cheers!"

We all sat down and immersed ourselves in pleasant
conversation. I was eager to learn as much about my hosts
as I could. But when they learned I was from California,
they only wanted to know about the beaches, the
weather, and the many things they had heard.

"Is it true that it never rains there?" Reiner asked.

Sadly, I had to dispel all myths. They seemed disappointed.

Then, Ilona excused herself for a moment as we continued to talk. When she returned, she said, showing her
warm smile, "You must stay for dinner."

"Oh, no," I said. "We can't do that."

She walked over to me, bent over as she lightly touched
my hands, and repeated it gently, "You must stay for
dinner."

"You mustn't argue," Reiner said with a smile. "She
always wins."

We were guided to the dining-room table, which was
now set for four. Reiner motioned for us to sit, and soon
Ilona appeared with a bowl of light soup for each of us. I
bowed my head and silently said grace. This was a habit I
had acquired as a child and now didn't seem like a time to
break it. I was truly thankful.

"Is everything okay?" Reiner asked.

"Yes," I replied with a broad smile. "Everything is perfect."

Ilona sat down, and we all began to eat. Then, as if on
schedule, she replaced our bowls with a course of roasted
turkey and gravy, accompanied by vegetables. The unique

flavor made me pause between bites to appreciate every taste. As I ate the last spoonful of my dinner, I was quite full—and satisfied. What a wonderful meal! I not only experienced a delicious dinner but I spent the evening with two giving people who opened their home—and their hearts—to two lonely American servicemen.

When we returned to the living room, we drank more wine, enjoyed more interesting chatter, and listened to soft music. Occasionally, Ilona would disappear into the kitchen for a few minutes, then return. Assuming she was cleaning, I offered my assistance. She brushed away the offer with a polite "No, thank you."

Then something sad happened—the night had to end.

"Would you like me to take you there?" Reiner asked.

"No," Chris answered. "It's a nice night."

"Moment," Ilona said as she ran into the kitchen.

She returned with two small wrapped baskets. Later, we'd discover they were filled with chocolates, cookies, and pastries. "This is for you," she said, presenting one to each of us.

As we bid the couple farewell, Ilona warmly said to me, "You welcome in our home anytime." I soon learned that wasn't just hollow politeness. There were more countless dinners, parties, and conversations over coffee and cake in our future. We all became very good friends.

That Christmas turned out to be the best I could have hoped for.

Lawrence D. Elliott

Oh, Christmas Tree

I grew up on the grounds of Folsom Prison, where my father worked for nearly two decades. During my childhood, trustees—inmates who were not considered a threat—were a constant; it was their responsibility to keep the grounds looking nice.

One January, I was sick and laying on the living-room couch, barely able to keep food down. In an adjacent room, our forlorn and very dried-out Christmas tree stood, awaiting removal. Mom had taken off the ornaments, but Dad had been too busy to drag the big tree out of the house.

Sitting on the couch and comforting me, Mom stared at the tree. She then stood up and went to the hallway, pulling several large sheets from the linen closet. She placed the sheets end-to-end, starting from the front door all the way to the huge tree. In total awe, I watched my mother wrestle and drag the very dead tree across the sheets to the front door. The tree shed nearly every needle onto the sheets during its journey. She then heaved the tree out the front door with great aplomb, throwing it onto the walkway.

By this time, I was off the couch, watching Mom and offering any moral support I could in my sickly state. She asked me to fetch a hammer. Dad never used a water stand for our Christmas tree but had "invented" his own stand, using two heavy wooden slats nailed to each other in an X-like fashion, with the middle then nailed to the base of the tree. Mom knew she had to remove the wooden stand for next year's tree.

The only hammer I could find in the junk drawer was a small one, which I took to her. With one foot atop the tree's trunk, Mom hit the wooden stand with the small hammer, to no avail. I stood in the doorway watching and cheering her on. It was then we heard a man's voice. Out in the street stood a trustee.

"Um, 'scuse me, Mrs. Johnson. Would you be needin' some help?" he asked. In his fifties or so, the trustee had a deep Southern accent.

Mom said yes, explaining that she was having trouble getting the wooden stand off, and that Mr. Johnson very much needed the stand for next year's Christmas tree.

"Why, I can fetch a bigger hammer from the shed and take that right off for ya," he responded. Mom thanked him and asked that he leave the stand on the front porch. I opened the screen door for her, and she started to come into the house.

"That's right fine, Mrs. Johnson," he said, then asked with some concern, "but when I get the stand off, where do you reckon Mr. Johnson wants me to plant the tree?"

At that point, Mom was facing me. She stared at me and told me with her "Mom eyes" to not even think about laughing. With all the grace she could muster, she turned around and said, "Why, that's okay. I don't think we'll use this tree next year for Christmas. If you could throw it in the trash, I would appreciate it."

"I've never heard of someone throwing away a

Christmas tree," the trustee said, shaking his head in disbelief. Then he asked, "Why, if it's okay with you and Mr. Johnson, can I have the tree?"

"Yes, you're welcome to it," Mom graciously replied.

With a huge smile on his face, and many "thank yous" in between, the trustee hoisted the brown and almost needleless tree over his shoulder and happily headed toward the prison's tool shed, promising to return the wooden stand in a few minutes.

When Mom came back into the house, we burst out with laughter as soon as she could close the front door. We laughed even harder picturing Dad's reaction had he come home to the tree expertly "planted" in his front yard. But, most importantly, our lifeless Christmas tree had brought joy to another and created a hilarious family Christmas story for generations to come.

Dahlynn McKowen

"It's for my mommy. Can you gift wrap a hug?"

The Morning Santa Came

A Christmas candle is a lovely thing;
It makes no noise at all,
But softly gives itself away;
While quite unselfish, it grows small.

Eva K. Logue

This Christmas was unlike any that I had ever known. The presents were under the tree arrayed in their majestic bows and shimmery wrapping paper. The nativity scene was proudly displayed, showing our tribute to the real meaning of Christmas. The snowmen boasted their presence all around the house. The only thing missing was us.

My husband and I work in a ministry for troubled teenagers. "Troubled" seems like such a nasty word— perhaps I should refrain from that and say, "Searching teenagers!"

Our boss had not spent Christmas with his family in six years, and now with two new grandchildren to celebrate with, it just seemed appropriate that this was the perfect year to spend Christmas away with his family. My husband and I were asked to spend the holiday with the students who could not go home for Christmas. It would be a sacrifice to break all family tradition, but one we were delighted to make.

I was not prepared for what this Christmas would have in store for us. I had already planned out the holiday feast menu and kept a variety of games to play. In the midst of singing Christmas carols, reading the Christmas story, making gingerbread houses, playing games, and feasting like kings, I felt as though there would be little time for quiet moments.

Every year since I was little, Santa had visited my grandparents' house. I always sat on his lap, and he would give me my present while camera flashes went off everywhere. This year, my special tradition would be broken. It was the first time in twenty-six years I would not sit on Santa's lap.

I went to bed on Christmas Eve thinking about our students. I began to put faces with stories, and it made me cry. These teenagers were searching for happiness, love, and hope. They were searching for someone to reach out to them—for someone to believe in them. I thought of the ones who had been victims of emotional, sexual, and physical abuse. Of those who had tried so many times to take their own lives. I thought of those who had never known the true meaning of Christmas, and of those who had never heard of the hope that the Savior brings.

I wanted them to wake up Christmas morning with joy and enthusiasm. I pulled something out of a bag that my grandma had given me. It was perfect. It was exactly what I needed to make this Christmas memorable. I ran my fingers over the velvet material, eagerly anticipating my plans.

The next morning couldn't arrive soon enough. I put on the velvet costume. My curly beard was a perfect match for my snow-white wig. I assembled the tray of hot cocoa and cookies and marched my way into the girls' dormitory.

"Ho, Ho, Ho!!!" I exclaimed as I flipped on the lights.

Gasps and laughs were heard throughout the dorm.

"It's Santa!!!" the teenage girls exclaimed.

Camera flashes filled the room. The girls eagerly came and posed for their pictures with Santa—bed heads and all.

The joy on their faces was unforgettable. They sat on the floor and ate their cookies while slowly sipping their hot cocoa.

We swapped Christmas stories, and then I asked, "What was your best Christmas?"

There were a variety of answers, but one answer left me heartbroken. One girl paused and then said, "By far, this one."

I've thought about those words over and over again. I didn't pass out lavish gifts. No one got amazing presents. It was the gift given from the heart that had made an impression—the love, the laughter, and the sacrifice.

Jennifer Smith

A Bottle of Cologne and a Handmade Handkerchief

The only gift is a portion of thyself.

Ralph Waldo Emerson

In 1948, it was our first Christmas in Houston.

My dad had only ever been fifteen miles away from his birthplace—except when he'd run away to join the Army—so he gave Mom an order: "We're going to Texas."

We left Connecticut in a 1937 Packard with a box of Mars Bars in the backseat to keep my brother, David, and me quiet while our tightly knit family waved a tearful good-bye from the country road that ran in front of our now sold house. The engine "fell out" in Stamford. The gas gauge went belly up in Pennsylvania, and our car coasted to a slow stop across from a huge hobo encampment. I can still see the dozens of fires and hear voices while the boxcar train whizzed past, filling the darkness with a mournful whistle. Dad told us to lock the doors while he walked to the little Pennsylvania Dutch town ahead to get help.

After what seemed like forever, we reached the out-
skirts of Houston, and my mom bent over double and
began to cry. This flat marshland was another world, so
different from green Connecticut. The smell of the stock-
yards gagged us. The belch of the oil refineries made our
eyes water. Soon, the inside of the car was a hiccupping,
sobbing mess.

Houston then, as now, was a booming town, with oil on
its mind. We rented two rooms in the back of a private
home. Mom, David, and I slept in the double bed, while
Dad slept beside us on a cot. One night, while eating a
hurried supper in the closet of our kitchen, we kept cool
by sitting in front of the open fridge until the landlord discovered us and threatened to kick us out. In the evening,
we wrapped wet washrags around our feet and plastered
them on our foreheads just to get a fugitive escape from
the unforgiving heat. At that time, there wasn't any refrig-
erated air, and only rich folks had attic fans. As the months
went on, hard times came upon us. Mom got work, which
left David and me totally alone. For the first time in our
lives, we had no close family, no aunties, no uncles—
nobody except each other. At school, the kids made fun of
our Yankee accents. We missed the woods, the green
fields, the freedom to run, and the peace that comes from
belonging to a family.

The weeks rolled into months. Christmas arrived. There
was no money for gifts, but David and I found a pretty,
almost empty bottle of cologne in a neighbor's trash can
and revived it by adding water, bay rum, and a few drops
of vanilla flavoring. We thought our concoction smelled
divine. I cut an overlarge square out of an old underslip,
hemmed it on four sides, and embroidered it with a shaky
"G" for George. It was a handkerchief for Dad. David
scrubbed it clean and wrapped it. On Christmas Eve, ours
were the only two presents under the little tree.

"You probably know already that we have no money for presents," Dad said with a choking voice. "But I am giving this very valuable two-dollar bill to you, Isabel. And David, I'm giving you your grandfather's pocket watch. Wind it carefully, and on the hour it will play a merry tune."

Visions of silver-white winter Christmases played in our heads—the huge spruces, all blue and silver, bedecked with candy, standing tall over hoards of presents, and our faraway family we missed unbearably. With an aching heart, I looked at my brother, and we both knew without speaking that it was time to treat our parents as if they had given us the most wonderful things in the world.

"This is a wonderful two-dollar bill," I said with as much certainty as I could muster. "What a wonderful Christmas!"

David just smiled broadly while he pressed his ear to the chiming watch. We all sat down by the tree, and our parents snuggled us close to them. When Dad opened his gift, it was the only time I ever saw him cry. Mom dabbed her new perfume behind her ears and declared that it smelled like heaven.

She kept that perfume bottle on her dresser for the next forty-eight years, and when I asked her about it years later, she looked at me with a wry twinkle in her eye and stated that it had always kept her in touch with true honesty. We buried Dad with his handkerchief. It was his only request.

Our lives improved. David and I matured, married, and had kids of our own. Many Christmases have come and gone since that one so many years ago, but none has ever matched it in the true spirit of the star in the East—a beacon home to love.

Isabel Bearman Bucher

A Cell-Phone Christmas

A cell phone is not the gift of choice for a woman who hates to talk on the phone. However, one Christmas, my husband, Dan, decided he could not make it through another year without a cell phone, so he thoughtfully bought one for me, too.

I tried to appear enthusiastic, but I'm not one of those people who enjoys phone conversations. As a training specialist at a government agency for twenty-seven years, I often responded to fifty phone calls per day. The last thing I wanted to experience again was the numbing sensation of an earpiece plastered to my ear.

Although my silver cell phone was as sleek and shiny as a new Corvette, it didn't turn me on. I didn't turn it on either, so I received very few calls at first, except from Dan. After a month or so, I began to toy with the phone and cautiously began to build a list of contacts and phone numbers. I followed the instruction guide as best I could, but with limited success.

The directions said to type in the phone number, save it, then push the letters to spell out the name. This sounded simple, but since the letters were in groups of three on the numbered key pad, the correct letter did not always appear on the screen. For instance, when I typed in the name of my son, Chuck, the screen read Achuck. I couldn't figure out how to delete the A, so I left it. Unfortunately, most of the names that ended up in my contact list had similar misspellings.

In the meantime, Dan gave his cell phone more attention than a new puppy. He played with it constantly, investigating every option on the menu. Then he called me to inform me of his latest discovery.

"Brring."

"Yes?"

"It's me. What are you doing?"

"I'm downstairs working on my column. What are you doing?"

"Oh, I'm upstairs playing with my new phone."

One day, Dan asked me for the phone number of my brother, Lester, in San Antonio. I told him to check the list of contacts on my cell phone. I knew I had put in Lester's name, although I didn't know what kind of weird spelling it might have.

Dan opened my cell phone, punched the menu button, and scrolled through the list of contacts.

"What kind of gibberish is this?" he said. "These names don't make any sense. Who is Any?"

"That's my friend, Amy."

"What about 'cellc'?"

"That's Candie's cell phone."

"Don't tell me you know someone named Faky."

"No, that was supposed to say Daly, but I couldn't make the D and L appear."

"I don't know how you recognize any of these names. Who is Frocel?"

"You know. Frolio's cell phone."

"Okay, let me guess. Inha must be Inga, and Kathyc is Kathy's cell phone."

"You're catching on now."

"And Maaahele is Michelle?"

"Right."

"I still can't find your brother, Lester. Wait a minute. Is he listed as Ester?"

"Yep. I couldn't get the L to pop up."

"This is like reading hieroglyphics. Tell me who mdjjjjj is."

"Oh, that's Melissa. At least, I got the M on her name."

"I give up on the next one. It's someone called Rally."

"That's easy. Rally is Sally."

Dan shook his head as he handed the cell phone back to me, laughing.

"As long as you can decipher who those names are, I guess it doesn't matter."

Since that day, I've added numerous other contacts to my phone, some spelled correctly and some spelled creatively. The cell phone turned out to be a valuable Christmas gift that I've grown to depend on, even if I occasionally tire of its ringing.

Oops, it's ringing right now. Who can it be? Uh huh, I should have known—just another call from my husband Fan.

Judy Lockhart DiGregorio

7

INSIGHTS
AND LESSONS

Make it a practice to judge persons and things in the most favorable light at all times and under all circumstances.

The Best Noël

At my company's holiday luncheon last year, our guest speaker, a pediatric neurosurgeon, presented a customer's perspective on the medical products our facility manufactures—implants for a neurological condition called hydrocephalus that affects mostly the very young and the elderly. All the employees, from line manufacturing personnel to top management, were able to see the impact on the world of the products they build by hand.

The 230 employees attending the luncheon had finished eating when Dr. Mike gave his presentation about the condition, its origin, prognosis, and treatment. He explained that the scientific community has a long way to go to understand and conquer this chronic, lifelong condition. It was very powerful in a way that made you wish you had paid more attention during Geometry and Trig, and that if you had you might have contributed an important piece to solve this enigmatic puzzle.

Throughout this festive holiday luncheon, the emcee would pull and call raffle-ticket numbers, and the winners would leap up to get their pick of some wrapped gifts on the front table. At these luncheons, winning is a big deal because the organizers don't skimp. A $100 gift card to Best Buy is not uncommon, and there are no rubber chickens.

Dr. Mike finished his talk by introducing a patient of his, a beautiful nine-year-old girl named Noël with long brown hair, deep brown eyes, and a smile that melted your heart. She had a way about her unlike a child of nine—or nineteen, for that matter—a wisdom of sorts that perhaps came from surviving a multitude of cranial surgeries, nights hooked up in hospitals, and mustering up positive energy for her parents when theirs finally ran out. Noël's mother stood up with her and imparted some very poignant words to the audience about their experience and their gratitude for the work put into designing and building this medical device that was working so well in her child. It had been implanted at a time when hope seemed scarce for her and her family. Her teary words of encouragement received a standing ovation.

Toward the end of the holiday program, Noël's raffle-ticket number got called. She lit up like any child would, staring at a table full of gifts wrapped with colorful paper and bows, and walked up to the front of the room by herself to select hers. Noël's selection was unknown to everyone, even her. She turned, facing the cheering people, and paused for a moment, looking at her wrapped prize, then lovingly at Dr. Mike. I remember thinking to myself, *She's unbelievably poised for a child her age.* Noël then raised her gift, took seven steps toward the surgeon who had skillfully changed her life when others before could not, and said, "I want you to have this gift, Dr. Mike." The cheering ceased, marked by the vacuous sound of air being rapidly inhaled by the audience, and then total silence at the realization of what was occurring. Dr. Mike didn't understand and turned to me with a puzzled look, so I said, "I think she wants to give you her gift!"

What child anywhere would do that? Noël. This child.

This angel. This tiny source of brilliant light knocked us all off our chairs with a gesture so uncommon and out of character for a child her age. She had the presence of mind to realize that she was holding something to offer the man who had given her back her life.

I've never witnessed a teammate hit a walk-off home run or catch a touchdown pass in overtime, but now I know what it feels like. Experiencing this moment was my best gift that year—maybe any year. Thank you, Noël.

Mark Geiger

Christmas Cookies

Stevie was barely five years old when he first came to visit, joining my youngest son and me for an afternoon of decorating Christmas cookies, which was a tradition in our home. We had done it ever since the oldest of our five children was small. Anticipating our afternoon, I arranged a Christmas tablecloth with bowls of icing, red and green sprinkles, and red and green colored sugars. I had baked cookies throughout the morning. Christmas carols were playing on the stereo. I wanted the boys to have a good time.

Stevie's eyes grew wide with excitement as he spied the table and its wares. I set trays of cookies in front of both boys. My son started spreading icing on the cooled cookies immediately. Stevie simply watched.

"Don't you like decorating Christmas cookies?" I asked him.

"I've never done it," he said. "I don't know how."

This was such a surprise to me, but then I knew that Stevie's mom was single and worked long hours. He was one of three small children, and there wasn't much money for extras in their home. His mom probably had just enough energy and money at the end of the day to put supper on the table and crawl into bed. Christmas cookies would be considered an extravagance.

I began slowly showing Stevie how to spread the white icing smoothly and evenly over each cookie. He laughed as we dusted sugar and sprinkles on the wet frosting. Soon Stevie had the hang of it and was busily decorating cookie after colorful cookie. Both boys had fun eating the confections, too.

"This is fun!" Stevie exclaimed repeatedly.

Somehow, I think I was the one having the most fun, watching my son teach his friend how to enjoy a new facet to the Christmas season.

"Can I come over and do this again?" Stevie asked.

"We'll plan another play date soon," I said.

There was as much icing and candy on Stevie as there was on the cookies and in the bowls! Perched atop a kitchen stool, his tongue deliberately wedged between his lips in strong concentration, Stevie decorated dozens of cookies. He didn't even notice when my son became bored and wandered off to watch a video.

"These are good," Steve said, biting a cookie he'd just decorated. "They're sweet."

When Stevie's mom came to pick him up, he was astonished that I was wrapping his decorated cookies and sending them home with him.

"To keep?" he asked.

"To eat!" I said.

Stevie left with his package of sweet Christmas cookies, and a face and shirt covered with evidence of how he'd spent the afternoon. His young mother was grateful for Stevie's fun afternoon and unique Christmas experience. I was left with a feeling of sheer joy at witnessing this little boy's first delight at decorating Christmas cookies, and knowing that we had, in a very small way, brightened Stevie's Christmas.

My children have always taken the cookie-decorating tradition for granted. They expect it every year, and as my son did this particular year, they typically grow bored after decorating just a few, and go off and find something else to do.

I was reminded this particular year just how richly our children are blessed, and how graced we are with the sweetness of cookies—and little boys. Traditions like baking Christmas cookies make for cherished memories.

I will hold our visit with Stevie among them.

Kimberly Ripley

The Truth About Christmas Decorations

Oh, sure, we all know that you can size up people pretty quickly by the way they dress, the kind of car they drive, and the company they keep. But, frankly, I think you never really know people until you see what kind of outdoor holiday decorations they display. Come December, people who don't so much as display a lawn ornament suddenly cover their entire yard with nativity scenes, pinwheel angels, and jumbo plastic candy. It's amazing, really.

Our neighbors, for example, are a nice, quiet, conservative couple who won't even leave their car parked on the driveway overnight. As of yesterday, they are the proud owners of five movable reindeer, a light-up tree, a sleigh, and a ten-foot inflatable snowman. Not that anything is wrong with this, mind you. I'm all for showing holiday spirit. But for as long as I've known them, there was nothing—*nothing*—about them that suggested something like this was coming.

But, really, I can see how this could happen. Christmas decorations, much like commercial jingles and, well, chicken pox, are contagious.

Consider our neighbors down the street. One year, they

bought a lovely outdoor Christmas tree with lights for their front yard. A few days later, eight wooden reindeer pulling Santa's sleigh appeared in front of the house next door. Then, shortly after that, a six-foot, fiber optic Frosty the Snowman showed up a few houses down, followed by a group of electronically animated elves singing "Jingle Bells" in the yard of the house across the street.

Coincidence? I don't think so.

However, one of the perks of holiday decorations is that you have an excuse to drive around and comment on other people's yards. But let me just warn you that sometimes this may only confuse and depress you. It's not because of the cold, but because, by a cruel twist of fate, some of the yards—the very same yards you've snubbed all year long—now look like something out of a Norman Rockwell painting, while yours has only a shoddy display of a tree made from a stack of aluminum cans!

Another thing about Christmas decorations, besides their obvious festive appeal, is that they tell us a great deal about the people who own them. I mean, you can tell who, exactly, is handy with a scroll saw, and who spends their weekends roaming around craft fairs. Or which family is deeply religious, and which is more of the gingerbread man type. In fact, there are a lot of houses in the neighborhood that we refer to by their Christmas decorations all year round. I mean, even in midsummer, the house around the corner is known as "the house with the blue icicle lights." In the house across from the park resides "the family who has a thing for ice-skating penguins."

And what about our house? Well, we put up our traditional Christmas display: lights-still-up-from-last-year. I'm not quite sure what this says about us, and, frankly, I don't want to know.

However, this year my husband has added three hand-crafted wooden reindeer. Of course, he claims it has nothing to do with our neighbor's elaborate display because "competing with friends over yard decorations is just plain silly."

With that said, when we came home today we noted they'd added a dozen plastic candy canes and a couple of polar bears.

Coincidence? Well, maybe.

But I'm not too worried about it—except for the fact that my husband just headed outside to measure our lawn for a full-sized Santa's workshop.

I just hope that January gets here soon.

Debbie Farmer

Secret Santa

I often remember the Secret Santa my mother invited into our lives. She introduced him to our family a number of years ago on Thanksgiving Day.

When Mom was hosting Thanksgiving at her house, she informed us we were going to do something a bit different that year. We were each going to play a Secret Santa from Thanksgiving until Christmas. All of us drew a name from a dish passed around and were instructed not to reveal the name we had chosen. Each person, from the youngest in the family to the oldest, was told they were now a Secret Santa to the person whose name they had drawn. A token gift would be given on Christmas Eve to reveal each other's Secret Santa.

We needed some innovation to keep our identity a mystery while we sent cards and small little trinkets as nominal gifts until Christmas Eve when we would once again gather as a family at my mom's house. Nothing particular was required of us as Secret Santas except to be unusually kind and nice to the person whose name we had drawn. We were not to reveal our identity, only to give suggestions on how to distribute kindness.

Then the fun began! Cards arrived from distance places,

and some contained little trinkets or pieces of gum or a sucker.

I was lucky enough to receive a little glass trinket in one of my envelopes. My Secret Santa knew of my interest and collections! Though my gift was not expensive crystal, it was a token from my Santa that let me know he or she was thinking especially of me.

As Christmas Eve drew closer, we began to suspect certain members of the family as they tried to fool us by both their kind and sly actions.

Some family members had a kinder Santa than others. Some received little; others more. Some postmarks originated from in state, and some from out of state. Mysteriously, though some family members lived out of state, it was not their postmarks that were found on cards! The suspense continued.

I, too, connived with people to mail my cards from distant places and schemed to fool my unsuspecting recipient of kindness. I put forth an effort to show love, thoughtfulness, and good will in innovative ways, while trying to determine my own Secret Santa with trickery and bribes.

As the days dwindled down, some knew for sure who their kindhearted friend or Secret Santa was—at least, they thought so. Other people were still awaiting their signs of good will. Other family members remained stumped at the benevolence shown them . . . could another family member actually be so kind?! Kindness and gifts given anonymously hold a thrill all their own. That year, and the succeeding years, left us each with a deep-seated feeling of consideration for others.

Christmas Eve arrived, and anticipation was in the air. Everyone was accusing all the others of ignoring or lavishing them with kindness. Some felt cheated and stated so, while others felt the generosity poured at their feet.

By the time gifts were given out at the beginning of the evening from the Secret Santas, all were cheering to play it again the next year. Some promised to be better in their distribution of kindness, and all were laughing and joking at the scheming that had occurred.

We repeated the game of Secret Santa for a few more years, but time evolved, people moved away, and new traditions were started.

Sometimes, when I remember the Secret Santa game, I think it should not take a game to promote kindness, but if it does, we should all play twelve months out of the year.

Betty King

A Secondhand Christmas

In the winter of 1975, my parents divorced. My mother had a chronic heart condition that made it impossible for her to work, and the two of us couldn't quite make ends meet that first year on our own.

In previous years, Christmas had been a grand event in our home. Money had always been scarce, but my parents scrimped and saved for the holidays.

My first memories are of bright lights, rich smells, and a pile of gifts with my name on them. That year, however, would be different. My mother received a meager Social Security check each month that almost, but not quite, covered the bare essentials, with nothing left for the luxuries of Christmas.

I remember that most of our meals consisted of potatoes and the big blocks of American cheese that the government passed out at the Social Security office. My mother, alone for the first time in her life, found it difficult to put aside her own hurts and fears and participate in the holidays. I do remember that we had a small tree and brought a box of decorations down from the closet shelf, but there wasn't much joy in our home that year.

One thing that did worry my mother was the lack of

money for gifts that year. She fretted over this for weeks, but there were no funds for presents. One day, a neighbor told her about a local toy charity, an organization dedicated to providing donated presents for children in need. My mother applied for the program and visited their office, bringing home a small box of gifts that she wrapped and hid under her bed.

The night before Christmas, we ate our baked potatoes, and Mom read to me from a book of children's Christmas stories. Just before bedtime, there was a knock at the door, and my mother answered to find a young woman who had just moved in next door to us. She was Hispanic, spoke very broken English, and had twin sons who were my own age.

She was also divorced and was in financial straits as bad as, or worse than, our own. She came to the door asking to borrow some flour, and she looked so exhausted that my mother invited her in and made her a cup of tea. I was hustled off to bed, lest I still be up when Santa made his appearance, and they stayed up and talked awhile.

I remember my mother coming into my room later and gently waking me up. Sitting on the side of my bed, she asked if I minded if we had company for Christmas. I said no, unused to voicing my opinion in such matters.

Then she took my hand and asked if it would be all right if Santa gave some of my presents to the two little boys next door. I thought about this for a while, wondering why Santa couldn't bring them their own presents, but somehow my young brain sensed that it would make my mother happy. She hadn't seemed happy in a long while, so I hesitantly agreed. Mother kissed my forehead, and I went back to sleep.

The next morning, I awoke to the most wonderful smell wafting under my bedroom door. Hunger banished even the memory of Christmas from my mind, and I ran from my room to the kitchen to find the source of that glorious aroma. I skidded to a stop as I rounded the corner into a strange, dark-faced woman standing at my mother's stove. She was rolling out tortillas and dropping them into a smoking pan, while a large pot bubbled noisily on the back burner.

I blinked once or twice in confusion until my mother walked in, then remembered that we had company, and even more importantly, that today was Christmas! I spun on my heels and ran into the living room to look under the tree. Two little Mexican boys sat, looking uncertainly around them, on our couch. Several small wrapped packages lay beneath the tree.

Mom followed me in and began to pass out presents. There were just enough for one gift each. I gazed longingly at the brightly wrapped packages in these strangers' hands, knowing I had almost possessed them, and clutching my solitary present tightly to my chest.

I unwrapped the box to find a G.I. Joe action figure, the old-fashioned kind with the moving knees and elbows. It usually came with a little rifle and backpack, and a string that you pulled to make him say cool army things, but mine didn't have a rifle or a backpack, and there was only a hole in the back where the string had once been. I stood there in the middle of the living room, my lip trembling, clutching my broken toy.

I looked to see what the other boys had received, the gifts I had missed out on. One package revealed a cap pistol (without caps) and a worn plastic holster (I had a much nicer set in the toy box in my room). The second box revealed a plastic bag full of Legos in various shapes and sizes. I stood there and watched these two boys whooping and laughing like these were the only toys they had, turning their meager gifts over and over in awe, and suddenly I realized that these *were* the only presents they had.

Soon, I would learn that these two, who would become my closest pals, each had exactly two shirts, two pairs of pants, and a worn sleeping bag that they shared on the floor of their room.

As I watched my mother talking to this strange woman in our kitchen, tears running down their cheeks, I was suddenly happy that she had woken me up, that Santa had shared my presents with these boys. How terrible would it have been to wake up with nothing under the tree, no presents to play with, no Santa at all?

The boys, Jay and Julio, followed me to my room, where I showed them, to their amazement, the wealth of my toy box.

Soon we were playing like old friends, until we were called out for a breakfast of seasoned eggs and potatoes wrapped in fresh, warm tortillas. I ate the best breakfast I could ever remember.

I'll never forget that morning, as I'll never forget my friends from Mexico who taught me there is always something to be thankful for, often much more than we think.

Perry P. Perkins

I Remembered Anthony

*Keep a good heart. That's the most
important thing in life. It's not how much
money you make or what you can acquire.
The art of it is to keep a good heart.*

Joni Mitchell

I maneuvered easily through the Wal-Mart parking lot, congratulating myself on my wisdom in avoiding the day-after-Thanksgiving rush. It wasn't much busier than a typical Saturday, and I was grateful that I had avoided the first day of Christmas shopping frenzy.

Three Marines were standing in front of the store, collecting for the Toys for Tots drive. Their crisp, perfectly tailored uniforms reminded me of my Marine son-in-law who had spent so much time away from my daughter and grandchildren serving his country. This year, he would not be home for Christmas.

"Have a good day, Ma'am," the Marine closest to me said in reply to my smile.

"You do the same," I said, thinking about my son-in-law, but also about how sad it is when kids have so little. Some of us complain about our wants, and yet we have so much. My own children never did without gifts and probably had more than they needed.

My mind wandered as I approached the front entrance, and the electric doors parted. As I walked through, I felt a tug of sadness as I wondered just for a moment, *What if I couldn't give my children anything? Or what if my grandchildren had no gifts for Christmas?* The thought made me unusually sad, considering it was a gloriously beautiful day and terrific for shopping. I grabbed a shopping cart and made a note at the end of my long shopping list to pick out an appropriate gift to drop in the box on my way out.

After a two-hour, five-lap tour around the huge store, my list dwindled to one small item dangling at the end: Christmas Gift—Toys for Tots. I wheeled toward the bulging toy aisles, stalking the perfect gift—a soft, cuddly doll for a little girl. Quickly, a darling Cabbage Patch Doll that would stay nestled in the arms of a little girl graced the top of my mounded shopping cart.

I headed toward the checkout, but my shopping cart made an abrupt stop. I stood in front of the display feeling a sense of urgency, as if I was forgetting something. I looked at the enticing boxes of race-car tracks, and suddenly I remembered—Anthony.

Over twenty-five years ago, six-year-old Anthony, his little sister Cassie, his mother, and his aunt lived in the tiny duplex next door to us. They didn't live there long—perhaps four or five months, extending through Christmas. It was long enough to note that things were difficult for the family. They lived modestly, and it wasn't unusual to find them without electricity in response to unpaid power bills. I tried to do what I could, but it wasn't much. I tried harder not to judge as I noticed that cigarettes and beer seemed the only things not in short supply.

That Christmas, like others, my children were up early

opening gifts, scampering around the neighborhood, and showing off their loot. As I passed my traditional array of holiday baked goods across the fence to my neighbors, Cassie strutted by with her new baby doll in a stroller. Anthony, smiling proudly, waved his only Christmas gift—a race-car track. While my own kids went from gift to gift as each lost its momentary thrill, these two kids spent hours on Christmas day playing with their beloved toys. I was surprised when one of my children noticed and announced somberly, "Mom, they only got one toy."

The following day, I was drawn by a bit of commotion outside. I stepped outside to see Anthony's mother put a box in the backseat of the car. Anthony stood there crying as the car pulled away. I wasn't sure what had happened until my six-year-old daughter clarified it later.

"Mom, Anthony told me his mom took his race car back to the store!"

"Really, why?"

"She said that they needed the money."

"Did they take Cassandra's doll back, too?"

"No, just Anthony's."

Later, I saw Anthony sitting on their front porch with his hands folded and his eyes staring down at the cracked concrete below his feet while Cassandra played in the grass with her doll. The little boy looked up, and his eyes mirrored the depth of heartbreak and disappointment he had already faced in his six short years of life. My husband and I talked about going out and buying him another race-car track, but even if we found room on our overextended credit cards, it was likely that it would end up for sale at the swap meet or returned stealthily to the store for a refund. Instead, my husband took his own slot-car set that was only a couple years old and in perfect condition and gave it to him. Anthony smiled when he saw the racetrack, but I know it didn't make up for the disappointment of having his gift returned.

That evening, our family discussed in-depth the new revelation to our children: not everyone has a pile of presents under their tree. They were shocked and sad that this little boy had received only one gift, and then it was taken away. As parents, we were sad that we could not explain or fix the situation. Occasionally, I thought about Anthony and how the challenges of his young years might have affected him. Did they make him bitter or stronger?

I decided then that every year at Christmas I would make sure we did something to honor the children who might not get a gift. We gave to individual families that we heard about or gave through church or various organizations, like Angel Tree and Toys for Tots. I did this for several years, but over time, our children grew up, married, and had children of their own, and life seemed to race forward one holiday to the next.

Several years had passed since I had made an effort to support a needy child at Christmas with a gift. True, I donated monetarily and gave food, but I had forgotten about the gifts. I had forgotten about Anthony.

So, there I stood in front of that display, with years of Christmas memories dancing around those boxes of race cars. There was only one thing left to do. I made a few tactical adjustments in the contents of my overflowing shopping cart and then deposited one huge box containing a race-car track next to the baby doll and headed toward the checkout.

As I left the store, one of the young Marines helped me put the boxes in the bins just outside the door. "Thank you very much, Ma'am. Have a happy holiday."

"It's a pleasure," I replied. "It's for Anthony." Then I gave him a slightly embarrassed smile and said to myself, *It's really nothing. I should do more. I should always do more.*

"Oh, and by the way, young man, have a very Merry Christmas!"

Valerie J. Frost

Christmas Memories in a Hospital

Thousands of glistening lights on a gigantic Christmas tree brighten the sky. Toy soldiers surround the entry, and it looks enchanting! However, this is not your typical building. It is a hospital—Children's Medical Center (CMC) of Dallas—where many children are extremely sick. As we enter, I think it must be a place filled with hopelessness and despair.

I fight back tears as we admit my daughter. Rebekah has cystic fibrosis and is hospitalized often. However, now she has double pneumonia and bronchitis and might be hospitalized through Christmas. My daughter must be on strong antibiotics and receive breathing treatments to clear her congested lungs. But how can she stay in the hospital during December? I am distraught as I focus on all of the activities she will miss. Will she get well enough to go home in time for Christmas?

Christmas is a time of celebration! My family has wonderful traditions in December. But since Rebekah is in the hospital, how can we celebrate? She will miss family parties, school festivities, last-minute shopping, decorating our tree, and the candlelight Christmas Eve celebration at our church. I am depressed as my husband, Nolan, and I take

Rebekah's personal belongings to the small sterile room that will be her home for the next ten to fourteen days.

Nurses immediately enter Rebekah's room to calm her fears and begin the strong medications. My daughter amazes me with her smiles and jokes with nurses and respiratory therapists, despite the fact that she is so sick. Nurses decorate the room with tinsel and open the curtains to show our daughter the Christmas tree and lights below. Rebekah is thrilled and proclaims, "This is the most perfect room." Her courage brings tears to my eyes because she is so determined to make the best of the situation.

During the next few days, family and friends begin arriving at the hospital, bringing encouragement and Christmas cheer. Rebekah receives numerous cards and calls. My sister, Sharron, brings a miniature Christmas tree with twinkling lights, as well as tiny decorations and videos for Rebekah to watch. Randy, my brother, sends a huge floral arrangement. Christmas music on a tape player allows us to listen to holiday music all day long. My son, Bryant, lets his little sister win game after game, much to her delight! My amazing daughter is joyful and appreciative of each act of kindness. But I still bemoan the many activities we are missing.

Family tradition is kept alive when my sister-in-law, Marilyn and my nieces arrive with cookies, icing, and colorful sprinkles for a cookie-decorating party. The cousins always decorate cookies together each Christmas, and this year the tradition continues, even in the hospital. The four cousins squirt each other with icing and vie to make the most creative cookie. Our family laughs and giggles, and I see for the first time that we can have fun—even in the hospital.

Nurses tell us that celebrities will be at the hospital the next week, but I don't really care. I just want to get Rebekah home! However, the pneumonia has a strong hold and keeps my courageous daughter in the hospital longer than anticipated. Sleepless nights, painful needles, and constant medications make the hospitalization difficult.

To our surprise, members of the Dallas Cowboys visit the hospital. Huge football players take time to attend a special event, meeting patients and talking with each child individually. Rebekah has her picture taken with Herschel Walker, Darryl Johnston, and Tony Casillas, just to name a few. And we are touched when Herschel carefully pulls children close to him for pictures. I wish everyone could see the gentle side of our sports heroes, who carefully hug sick children and talk in soft voices. For a few moments, sick children forget their pain and illnesses while celebrities focus on them. Tears stream down my face as I witness compassion and tenderness from the huge football players. These mighty players, who knock men to the ground during a game, joke with children who have tubes and IVs attached and ever so tenderly hug each child. For a moment, I forget we're in a hospital.

Other exciting events occur that help me understand the true meaning of Christmas. Another day, members of the Texas Rangers baseball team spend a morning autographing pictures and visiting with sick children. Also, numerous deliveries of toys and gifts are made to each room from a variety of businesses. Santa Claus surprises each child, and Christmas carolers comprised of police officers sing to the children. One day, fingernail painting and hair styling is provided by a group of beauticians. Rebekah chooses bright purple polish for her nails.

Through the Troy Aikman Foundation, a wonderful and educational entertainment room was recently completed. Aikman's End Zone features computers that allow hospitalized children to chat with kids in other children's hospitals around the nation. Rebekah loves spending time in the room, and especially communicating with other sick children. The staff at CMC is determined to create an environment to promote healing.

So, even though Rebekah is very sick, she is not bored. My daughter is filled with hope and happiness. In fact, through the efforts of volunteers, sports heroes, and dedicated doctors and nurses, Rebekah has an amazing attitude. One night, Rebekah says, "Mom, I feel so special because so many people help children in the hospital!"

Finally, we receive the good news that our daughter will get to go home on Christmas Eve. It is a miracle because, days earlier, her body had been ravished with fever and pneumonia. Now, she is well! My heart is filled with gratitude toward all who helped. God has healed Rebekah. And again I am thankful for the power of prayer to our great and mighty God.

Was it just the medications that healed her, or the hope, encouragement, and prayers she received from so many? All I know is that when we left the hospital, we looked back to see the same twinkling lights, enormous Christmas tree, and toy soldiers at the entrance. But now the hospital no longer seems a place of despair, but a place filled with hope, healing, and cherished Christmas memories.

Marilyn Phillips

The Sound & Spirit of Christmas Through the Ears of a Deaf Woman

Christmas is not just a day, an
event to be observed and speedily forgotten.
It is a spirit which should permeate
every part of our lives.

William Parks

Each June, Nashville plays host to thousands of fans, who descend upon Music City to meet their favorite superstars at the Country Music Association's Fan Fair. As John Berry's publicist at the time, I accompanied the country superstar to this event in 1997. Little did I know that the sound and spirit of Christmas would find me a little early that year.

In a booth resembling his front porch on his Georgia farm, John sat in a rocking chair inviting fans to do the same in another rocking chair beside him. As I stood to the side, silently observing the scene, fans filed onto the porch.

From that stream of fans, one very special woman would capture all of our hearts as she reminded us that the spirit of Christmas is not confined to any one time of year or place or type of sound. We onlookers witnessed a Christmas miracle as thousands of others swirled around us.

Her name was Mary.* Mary was deaf, with only the most microscopic traces of sound penetrating her quiet world. John was her favorite singer, and she had come to present him with a request unlike any he had ever received before. Although deaf, Mary's other sharpened senses allowed her to celebrate the world in a manner beyond the comprehension of most people. She absorbed music, not through the hearing world's intricate system of hammers, anvils, and stirrups, but rather through her fingertips.

As we watched, Mary sat in the rocking chair next to John and explained to him how she would gently put her hands on stereo speakers and experience his music through the vibrations.

In this surreal environment, amidst a whirlwind of a million flashbulbs, concerts, and autograph sessions, Mary asked for the greatest gift one person can give to another—the loving gift of self.

"Will you please sing 'O Holy Night' for me?" Mary requested in a humble voice, which had been trained long before her ears had gone silent. "It's my favorite song."

The classic Christmas song had long ago become one of John Berry's signature tunes.

Once John understood the enormity and unique nature of this request, he simply looked into Mary's eyes and replied, "I would be honored."

Closing her eyes, Mary gently placed her hands on John's throat. John gazed intently at his audience of one and, in his best a capella, began to sing the song that is traditionally reserved for Christmas Eve.

For privacy, the woman's name has been changed to Mary.

"O holy night, the stars are brightly shining. It is the night of our dear Savior's birth. . . ."

For us onlookers, Mary was what I call an earthly angel, who had been sent to teach us a lesson about the universal spirit of Christmas and living. Few words were spoken during those moments other than the unforgettable lyrics John was singing.

"Now long lay the world, in sin and error pining, till he appeared and the soul felt its worth. . . ."

I was merely a spectator, who was blessed, perhaps even divinely chosen, to stand in the larger audience surrounding the booth that day. We all stood quietly around the porch for this inspired performance, which was so removed from the revelry just a few feet beyond us.

Tears slipped from Mary's clutched eyes, gracefully sliding down over her cheeks. John's own eyes sent tears flooding forth as his powerful tenor voice held strong.

"A thrill of hope, the weary world rejoices, for yonder breaks a new and glorious morn. . . ."

As we watched, the strength and devotion of Mary touched each one of us in a special place deep within our souls. She granted us the privilege of being a part of her world for an exceptional instant. In those brief few moments, Mary allowed us to travel with her on an incredible journey to a sacred place and back, culminating with John's vibrant conclusion.

"Fall on your knees, oh hear the angel voices, oh night divine, oh night when Christ was born, oh night divine, oh night, oh night divine."

My mortal emotions silently beckoned for this moment to continue endlessly. However, these special moments, by mere design of nature, are not meant to last. I later grew to understand that these impermanent moments are meant to glimpse at and savor as they soar by us and through us like the shooting star that brilliantly blazes and then fades into ebony, bequeathing the fortunate viewer with an indelible impression and inspiration.

In the silence that followed, Mary opened her eyes and stared into John's eyes for a moment. Then she simply said, "Thank you," as she quietly stood and walked off the front porch, asking for nothing more.

John sat silently for a few moments, staring at Mary as she walked away.

As quietly and as unexpectedly as she had entered into each of our lives, Mary was once again enveloped by the immense crowd bustling back and forth in search of their own shooting stars.

I, too, would later blend into that crowd, but along with everyone else who had been swept away by Mary and John, I took with me an unlikely Christmas gift that afternoon. I learned that we need not experience the spirit of Christmas only on that day. Rather, it is with us every day if we open ourselves to experiencing and understanding these rare moments of inspiration.

Only fate knows if Mary and John and, indeed, the rest of us will ever cross paths again. The same divine fate that momentarily joined us suggests that we will not, but ours is a connection beyond this world now; it is a part of our eternal beings. Everyone who stood around that front porch in the sweltering heat on that long ago June afternoon in Nashville will forever share a precious bond for which we each, most especially Mary, gave one another a small piece of ourselves before traversing back into our individual worlds.

John E. Schlimm II

The Matchless Gift

Those who wish to sing always find a song.

Proverb

After my second graders completed reciting the "Pledge of Allegiance," they settled back in their seats. But Duane remained standing. Duane was an exceptionally bright and lovable student, but his home life was far from perfect.

His mother was a single parent who struggled with many personal problems. Duane and his three younger sisters were often taken by Social Services when life got too tough for her. Thinking that maybe he had had a bad night, I walked over to him to see what was the matter. As he looked up at me with dark brown eyes, I could see his hurt and disappointment.

"Mrs. Brown, aren't you going to open my Christmas present?" he asked. "I put it on your desk."

As I looked at my desk, all I could see was an avalanche of papers, stickers, and books. Seeing my puzzled look, Duane went to the front of the room and retrieved his gift from my desk. As he handed it to me, I noticed the wrapping paper was a napkin from the lunchroom. Carefully removing the napkin, my gift appeared to be a matchbox. Although I had only been a teacher for three months, I had learned the important lesson of asking a child to explain a picture or, in this case, a gift, instead of disappointing him with a wrong guess. So I asked Duane to tell me about his gift.

First, Duane instructed that I had to use my imagination before opening my gift. He then began to tell me that this wasn't really a matchbox, but a jewelry box. Inside, if I would use my imagination, I would find two precious gems.

As I opened my jewelry box, I was surprised by the sight as well as the smell of two beer caps. Duane informed me that, instead of beer caps, they were really two precious silver earrings. He had noticed that I never wore earrings and wanted me to have some pretty ones.

My eyes began to tear at the thoughtfulness of this child's precious gift. Since birth, one of my ears was slightly deformed. Fearing that wearing earrings might draw attention to the ear, I never wore them. But how could I not wear these precious earrings given by this special child? As I placed the earrings on my ears with masking tape, my class clapped, and Duane stood proudly beside me.

Every year after that, the matchbox remained on my desk. It reminded me of this child's kindness and the wonderful lessons he taught me. Much like the widow and her two mites, Duane gave all he had, his heart. Although his situation at home was not the best, Duane continued to see the good in life. The beer caps were an ugly reminder of some problems in his neighborhood, but Duane had made them into something beautiful—two precious gems. Although my ear was deformed, Duane still wanted me to have pretty earrings. Even though the matchbox had held the matches that lit cancer-causing cigarettes, his surprisingly tender heart allowed us all to see it as a treasure box instead of a dangerous weapon. Although Duane did not have much money, he still wanted to give. Whenever I see Duane's gift on my desk, it encourages me. If I am having trouble reaching a student, I try to be like Duane and give that student a piece of my heart. When I am having a trying day, one glance at the matchbox reminds me of the small boy who had a trying day every day but still could find the treasures among the trash.

Out of the good heart of a second-grade boy, one teacher will always have a gift to treasure. Many holiday seasons have come and gone, but the memory of my matchbox gift never fails to warm my heart or be extinguished from my mind.

May we never fail to let even the littlest souls teach us. They are more than willing to teach, but we must be willing to take the time to truly listen.

Stephanie Ray Brown

"Thank you, Charlie. A snowball and you
made it yourself! How thoughtful."

When Good Things Happen to Bad Children

*You can learn many things from children.
How much patience you have, for instance.*

Franklin P. Jones

When I remember my favorite Christmas gift as a young girl, I see a porcelain ballerina posed en pointe on an ivory and gold pedestal, with fragile arms softly framing her heart-shaped face. Wearing a short rose and cream tutu, she gazed at me from a store window as Mother and I shopped for Christmas.

At my insistence, we entered the small, musty store to examine her. The salesman informed us that the hand-painted ballerina wore a tutu of authentic cotton lace dipped in porcelain. The hand-sculpted pink flowers inset into her tutu and chestnut hair were exquisite. Such work made the figurine very expensive, but I begged my mother to buy her for Christmas, even if she were my only gift.

Each day, I asked my mother whether she had purchased the ballerina. "Wait until Christmas and find out," she replied.

Finally, Christmas was just one week away, and my

mother went grocery shopping, leaving me and my twelve-year-old brother, Charles, to mind the three younger children. The opportunity was too tempting to miss.

Charles didn't hesitate to use his authority to boss us around while Mother was absent, but, of course, since I was a cocky eleven-year-old, I ignored everything he said. To his horror, I announced my intention to find the hidden Christmas gifts and look for my ballerina.

The search began underneath my parents' double bed. Lifting up the chenille bedspread, I saw nothing but dust balls and a snoring cat. Then I peered into their bedroom closet and found only clothing and shoes. Finally, I grabbed a wooden stool and headed for the hall closet.

Behind the cotton blankets on the top shelf were several packages in brown paper bags. My heart began to race as I retrieved the bags one by one to investigate them. Charles warned me to stop and steadfastly refused to look into any of the bags himself. However, he reluctantly agreed to hold the stool while I reached for one last package on the highest shelf.

Suddenly, the phone rang, and Charles ran to answer it. As the stool tipped, I lost my balance, and the package in my hands hit the tile floor with a bang.

With my heart pounding, I carefully withdrew the white cardboard box inside the bag and opened it. Then I unfolded layers of crisp white tissue paper. Nestled in the bottom of the tissue was my dream gift, the porcelain ballerina I craved so desperately, but now she was a one-armed ballerina. The other one lay beside her.

"I knew that would happen," declared my brother.

"It's your fault her arm's broken," I wailed. "You shouldn't have let go of the stool when the phone rang."

Guilt, remorse, and panic overwhelmed me as I stared at the broken figurine. *What had I done? Could I glue the arm back on before my mother returned?*

This accident was partly her fault, I rationalized. She often peeked at her own Christmas gifts. Obviously, this was a genetic tendency. I had inherited her gift-peeking genes.

Mother returned from the store with a car full of grocery bags to find me weeping hysterically at the back door. I grabbed her skirt and instantly confessed my crime, begging her forgiveness.

"Oh, Judy," she cried. "When your father comes home, we'll see if he can glue the arm back on, but don't you dare look at any more Christmas gifts."

Gratefully, I nodded my head as I wiped my dripping nose on my sleeve, relieved that the catastrophe hadn't netted me worse punishment.

Somehow, my father managed to glue the arm back in place with the hairline fracture barely visible, and the Christmas gift disappeared once more from my sight.

The ballerina made her official debut on Christmas morning, much to my relief and joy. I tenderly removed her from her wrappings and gazed at the delicate beauty that had almost been destroyed by my childish impatience.

She promptly took a position of honor atop a crocheted doily on my scratched-up mahogany dresser. There she remained for many years, a vivid reminder that occasionally, at least, good things happen to bad children.

Judy Lockhart DiGregorio

In-Law Survival Hot Line

This is my Christmas nightmare come true—my husband, David, our two-year-old, our newborn, and I crammed into David's sister's spare bedroom for the Christmas holidays. Our routine is topsy-turvy. No one can sleep. Molly won't nurse. Haley throws potty-training right out the window.

The house is impeccably decorated and far from child-proof. Breakable Christmas decorations fairly call to Haley from every nook and cranny. The conversations are about people I don't know and inside jokes I don't get. With no sleep, I feel like I could cry at any minute. To make matters worse, David is magically transported back to his child-hood, when his mother and sisters catered to his every whim—forgetting that his wife and kids are even here.

My in-laws' unsolicited advice is flying at me from every direction. Haley is contending with a new sibling and a very nervous mother. David's family enthusiastically sup-ports spanking. This feels like parenting on a stage in front of opening-night critics.

As David sits at one end of a sumptuous dinner (none of which Haley recognizes or is willing to taste) with his mother and sisters worrying that he's not sleeping or eat-ing well at home, I am forgotten on the other end, with

Molly in my arms and Haley squirming on one knee. Molly starts to cry. I excuse myself to nurse her and, as if on cue, opinions begin ricocheting off the walls.

"That baby can't be hungry. You just fed her."

"You're going to spoil her if you pick her up so much."

"How do you even know anything is coming out when you nurse her?"

I politely thank them and try again to escape.

That's when Haley makes a puddle on my sister-in-law's new carpet. And here we go again.

"She's too young to be potty-trained. Just stick her back in diapers and let her be a baby a while longer."

"Are you kidding? Mine were all potty-trained by that age."

I'm about to cry. I apologize about the carpet, grab Haley and the baby, and excuse myself to a back bedroom.

I indulge myself with a good, long cry. I can still hear the forum outside.

"Why don't we just buy her some formula? She might want some later."

"It's her baby. Let her feed her what she wants to feed her. We could buy some diapers, though."

That's when the answer hit me: The Holiday In-Law Survival Hot Line. This is how it works. When you just can't take it any more—when you've smiled, bitten your tongue, and feel as if you might explode—you slip away to a telephone and dial. An automated voice details the options: "If your mother-in-law has just offered to teach you to cook your husband's favorite meals, press 1. If she claims to have potty-trained all her kids by age one, press 2. If your perfect sister-in-law and her perfect husband have just arrived with their two perfect children, press 3. If your mother-in-law has come over for a holiday dinner and just pulled out your washer and dryer to clean behind them, push 4."

The hot-line volunteers will be seasoned veterans of the in-law infantry—women who've been through it and lived to tell about it. They'll listen sympathetically and offer a gentle, "Hon, just kill them with kindness and pray they leave soon."

"Hey, if the woman wants to clean behind your dryer, point her to your refrigerator, too."

"Sugar, you don't really want to strangle your husband, do you?"

* * *

Here it is, New Year's Eve with my own family—normal people at last. Seventy-some loud, hearty Cajuns all talking at once, laughing and, as we say in Louisiana, "Passing a good time." I see my sweet, little sister-in-law, pregnant and green around the gills. She stands with her toddler on her hip as two of my sisters toss her advice.

"You'd better get that baby out of your bed or you'll soon have four of you in there. I'll tell you what you do . . ."

I look at my sister-in-law, at her frozen, polite smile, her desperate scan of the room to locate my brother. Suddenly, it hits me. We are the in-laws! I am an in-law. I'd never seen things through my sister-in-law's eyes before—spending the holidays with her husband and his huge, boisterous family.

Aha, a potential hot-line volunteer, I think. I pull my sister-in-law aside to recruit her. "How'd you like to serve on the board of directors for a new 800 hotline I'm organizing? You'd be perfect. . . ."

Mimi Greenwood Knight

A Lesson in Forgiveness

*Apology is a lovely perfume; it can transform
the clumsiest moment into a gracious gift.*

Margaret Lee Runbeck

It was snowing as I finished unbuckling my baby from her car seat. A toot from behind reminded me that I was holding up traffic on the one-way street.

I didn't care. My six-month-old had to get an immunization shot, which meant she would be up all night with a fever. My head ached like I was coming down with the flu, and my husband's job didn't look steady for the holidays. I wasn't in a good mood.

The truck tooted its horn again. When I finally had my little one in my arms and covered from the cold air, I looked up and felt my heart sink. I had inadvertently parked in a delivery zone. A look at the name printed on the truck confirmed that I was parked in his place.

Angry at myself for not noticing the sign sooner, I put my baby back into the car and looked down the street. The nearest empty place was more than a block away. Gritting my teeth, I was tempted to go home and reschedule my baby's vaccination for a day when things were going better, but I didn't.

After managing to parallel park in a tight spot, I again got ready to get out of my car. Glancing up, I saw someone waiting for me outside. I knew it was the truck driver. Bracing myself for a verbal attack, I slowly emerged from the car.

"Sorry about that back there." A strong note of apology rang in the man's voice. I looked at him suspiciously. He was actually grinning at me!

"I saw you had a baby," he continued, "but there wasn't any other place big enough for me to park in."

I managed to stammer my own apology, although I was completely taken aback by his friendly manner. Like Scrooge, I wondered if this was a setup.

"I'd like to give you this." The stranger held out a coffee mug with his company's name on the side. He didn't wait for my reply but shouted, "Merry Christmas!" and sprinted away as fast as he dared on the slick pavement.

I stared after him, the coffee mug still in my hand. As the snow continued to fall steadily around me, a warm feeling spread throughout my body, and I smiled for the first time all day.

At home, that coffee mug serves as a constant reminder to me of the way that driver showed unexpected kindness and forgiveness to me that day. As I drink from it each day, it also reminds me of the way God forgives each of us when we least deserve it.

Using the coffee mug each morning as I begin my day inspires me to work on showing that same kindness and forgiveness to everyone I meet—clerks, cashiers, complete strangers—not just at Christmas, but every day of the year.

Kayleen Reusser

More Chicken Soup?

Many of the stories you have read in this book were submitted by readers like you who had read earlier *Chicken Soup for the Soul* books. We publish at least ten or twelve *Chicken Soup for the Soul* books every year. We invite you to contribute a story to one of these future volumes.

Stories may be up to 1,200 words and must uplift or inspire. You may submit an original piece, something you have read or your favorite quotation on your refrigerator door.

To obtain a copy of our submission guidelines and a listing of upcoming *Chicken Soup* books, please write, fax, or check our website.

Please send your submissions to:

Website: *www.chickensoup.com*
Chicken Soup for the Soul
PO Box 30880, Santa Barbara, CA 93130
fax: 805-563-2945

We will be sure that both you and the author are credited for your submission.

For information about speaking engagements, other books, audiotapes, workshops, and training programs, please contact any of our authors directly.

Supporting Others

With each Chicken Soup for the Soul book we publish, we designate a charity to receive a portion of the profits. A portion of the proceeds from *A Chicken Soup for the Soul Christmas* will be donated to the Unity Shoppe in Santa Barbara, California.

Drs. Pearl Chase and Hazel Severy began the work as a Holiday Program in 1917. They were concerned for all the low-income families, their children, and the elderly who needed some assistance during the holiday season. The town was small and the gifts simple! They began by coordinating the efforts of all those who wanted to help.

Barbara Tellefson began her volunteer commitment in 1974. She listened to the needs of the poor and developed the program into a year-round effort. Other non-profit agencies worked together to avoid duplication of services. This made it possible for every agency to refer their qualified low-income clients to one location so everyone could be helped with better and more consistent services throughout the year.

In January 2004, Barbara Tellefson stepped down as executive director of the agency after thirty years of service. Tom Reed, the director of development, was hired as the new executive director. Barbara Tellefson continued to assist his efforts as the director of operations. Tom Reed heads the small staff of 14 employees and more than 7,000 volunteers who assist the agency throughout the year. Yearly 1,500 local children volunteer to operate the Free Stores as they learn merchandising, inventory control, bar coding, and customer service skills for future job opportunities.

Kenny Loggins, Jeff Bridges, Peter Noone, and many area celebrities joined the local TV station (KEYT3/ABC) to produce a local Holiday Telethon to raise funds. This tradition makes it possible for the agency to purchase some of the needed food supplies, clothing, school supplies, and holiday toys at wholesale closeout prices. This "Free Store" makes it possible for clients to shop for their needs with dignity.

With the help of the community and Pierre Claeyssens, two buildings were purchased to collect inventory and barcode $2 million in merchandise yearly. Today, more than 250 other charities refer their clients for year-round services. Over 65,000 visits are made annually to the Central Distribution Facility!

The Unity Shoppe is now the single largest direct distributor of food, clothing, and toys in Santa Barbara County. The Unity Shoppe receives no city, county, state, federal, or United Way funding. They rely on the generosity of the community and the thousands of donors who have heard of their work.

For more information, please visit the website at www.unityshoppe.org or call or write to:

Unity Shoppe, Inc.
1219 State Street
Santa Barbara, CA 93101
(805) 965 4122

Who Is Jack Canfield?

Jack Canfield is the cocreator and editor of the *Chicken Soup for the Soul* series, which *Time* magazine has called "the publishing phenomenon of the decade." The series now has more than 140 titles with over 100 million copies in print in forty-seven languages. Jack is also the coauthor of eight other bestselling books including *The Success Principles™: How to Get from Where You Are to Where You Want to Be, Dare to Win, The Aladdin Factor, You've Got to Read This Book,* and *The Power of Focus: How to Hit Your Business, Personal and Financial Targets with Absolute Certainty.*

Jack has recently developed a telephone coaching program and an online coaching program based on his most recent book *The Success Principles.* He also offers a seven-day Breakthrough to Success seminar every summer, which attracts 400 people from about fifteen countries around the world.

Jack is the CEO of Chicken Soup for the Soul Enterprises and the Canfield Training Group in Santa Barbara, California, and founder of the Foundation for Self-Esteem in Culver City, California. He has conducted intensive personal and professional development seminars on the principles of success for more than a million people in twenty-nine countries around the world. Jack is a dynamic keynote speaker and he has spoken to hundreds of thousands of others at more than 1000 corporations, universities, professional conferences, and conventions and has been seen by millions more on national television shows such as *Oprah, Montel, The Today Show, Larry King Live, Fox and Friends, Inside Edition, Hard Copy,* CNN's *Talk Back Live, 20/20, Eye to Eye,* and the *NBC Nightly News* and the *CBS Evening News.* Jack was also a featured teacher in the hit movie *The Secret.*

Jack is the recipient of many awards and honors, including three honorary doctorates and a Guinness World Records Certificate for having seven books from the *Chicken Soup for the Soul* series appearing on the *New York Times* bestseller list on May 24, 1998.

To write to Jack or for inquiries about Jack as a speaker, his coaching programs, trainings, or seminars, use the following contact information:

Jack Canfield
The Canfield Companies
PO Box 30880 • Santa Barbara, CA 93130
phone: 805-563-2935 • fax: 805-563-2945
E-mail: info4jack@jackcanfield.com
www.jackcanfield.com

Who Is Mark Victor Hansen?

In the area of human potential, no one is more respected than Mark Victor Hansen. For more than thirty years, Mark has focused solely on helping people from all walks of life reshape their personal vision of what's possible. His powerful messages of possibility, opportunity, and action have created powerful change in thousands of organizations and millions of individuals worldwide.

He is a sought-after keynote speaker, bestselling author, and marketing maven. Mark's credentials include a lifetime of entrepreneurial success and an extensive academic background. He is a prolific writer with many bestselling books, such as *The One Minute Millionaire, Cracking the Millionaire Code, How to Make the Rest of Your Life the Best of Your Life, The Power of Focus, The Aladdin Factor,* and *Dare to Win,* in addition to the *Chicken Soup for the Soul* series. Mark has had a profound influence on many people through his library of audios, videos, and articles in the areas of big thinking, sales achievement, wealth building, publishing success, and personal and professional development.

Mark is the founder of the MEGA Seminar Series. MEGA Book Marketing University and Building Your MEGA Speaking Empire are annual conferences where Mark coaches and teaches new and aspiring authors, speakers, and experts on building lucrative publishing and speaking careers. Other MEGA events include MEGA Info-Marketing and My MEGA Life.

He has appeared on *Oprah,* CNN, and *The Today Show.* He has been quoted in *Time, U.S. News & World Report, USA Today, New York Times,* and *Entrepreneur.* In countless radio interviews, he has assured our planet's people that "you can easily create the life you deserve."

As a philanthropist and humanitarian, Mark works tirelessly for organizations such as Habitat for Humanity, American Red Cross, March of Dimes, Childhelp USA, and many others. He is the recipient of numerous awards that honor his entrepreneurial spirit, philanthropic heart, and business acumen. He is a lifetime member of the Horatio Alger Association of Distinguished Americans, an organization that honored Mark with the prestigious Horatio Alger Award for his extraordinary life achievements.

Mark Victor Hansen is an enthusiastic crusader of what's possible and is driven to make the world a better place.

Mark Victor Hansen & Associates, Inc.
PO Box 7665 • Newport Beach, CA 92658
phone: 949-764-2640 • fax: 949-722-6912
www.markvictorhansen.com

Contributors

Martha Ajango taught first grade for thirty-one years in Fort Atkinson, Wisconsin. She has written "Messages Everywhere," a collection of short, inspirational vignettes about how she discovers God in commonplace experiences. Please e-mail her at majango@charter.net.

Jennie Spencer Baty was born and raised in Escalante, Utah, and completed her degree in education and english at the University of Utah in the early 1960s. She has devoted her life to teaching, writing, and being an inspiring mother. She has published a book, *Twin Rivers*, and has written many poems and other stories.

Lisa Beringer is a piano teacher who writes inspirational stories, humorous plays, and daily e-mails to her four children who have spread their wings and left the nest. She lives with her husband, Dale, in Ontario, Canada, where they enjoy fishing aboard *Audacious* and acting together in their church family drama troupe.

Lyla Berry, Ed.D, MPM, RN has enjoyed a career that encompasses extensive experience in both nursing and education including articles, textbook, DVD and CD on various aspects of nursing. Retired, she continues to write, loves cooking (section editor, *Red Hat Cookbook*), gardening, and lectures as a Humorist. lyla.b@verizon.net.

Lynnea Bolin is a ten-year-old student who attends fifth grade at Thomas Jefferson Elementary School. Lynnea enjoys reading, writing, drawing, animals, soccer, and dance. She also enjoys taking care of her two dogs and her guinea pig. Lynnea's inspiration is her sister Lylian, who writes novels about horses.

Amy Breitmann received her B.S. in Education and M.A. in Counseling from Bowling Green State University in 1994. She is one of the founders of the Lydia Project, Inc., a nonprofit agency supporting women facing cancer. She enjoys writing, teaching, and camping with her family. Contact Amy at development@the lydiaproject.org.

Janet K. Brennan is a poet and author living in the foothills of Albuquerque, New Mexico. She attended the University of New Hampshire, Hesser Business College, and has a legal certificate from the University of New Mexico. Janet has authored poetry and short stories, which have been published around the world, and has recently had two books of her own released. Janet has just completed a novel and is getting ready to release a book of serialized short stories about the west. Visit Janet's website at www.jbstillwater.com.

Stephanie Ray Brown loves to make holiday memories with family, especially with all the clan that gathers at her Granny's small house in Providence, Kentucky. Every memory made is precious and treasured, just like "The Matchless Gift" she received as a first-year second-grade teacher. After being blessed to be a stay-at-home mother to Savannah and Cameron for twelve years, Stephanie has recently returned to teaching as a part-time reading instructor at Niagara Elementary in Henderson, Kentucky.

Isabel Bearman Bucher is a freelance writer. She is a mother to Erica and Shauna, splendid young women, wife to Robert, sister, and friend. From this fertile field comes her stories of the heart. She's author of two books. *Nonno's Monkey* will soon be on the web at www.oneitaliana.com.

Joan Clayton is the author of eight books and is a religion columnist for her local newspaper. In 2003, she was named Woman of the Year in her town. Joan has been in *Who's Who Among America's Teachers* three times. She and her husband are retired educators. Her e-mail address is joan@yucca.net.

Beth Copeland is an English and creative writing instructor at East Carolina University. Her poetry book, *Traveling Through Glass*, received the 1999 Poetry Book Award from Bright Hill Press.

Cookie Curci was born during WWII and most of the articles she writes about are from in and around that time frame. For sixteen years she wrote a popular nostalgia column for her community newspaper, *The Willow Glen Resident* (The Silicon Valley Metro Newspapers . . . San Jose California). Her generational stories have appeared in several nostalgia books and newspapers across the country.

Michele Ivy Davis is a freelance writer whose stories and articles have appeared in a variety of magazines and anthologies, as well as in newspapers and law-enforcement publications. Her young adult novel, *Evangeline Brown and the Cadillac Motel*, was published by Penguin and has won national and international awards. Learn more about her at www.MicheleIvyDavis.com.

Judy Lockhart DiGregorio is an Army brat from San Antonio, Texas, who now lives in Oak Ridge, Tennessee. She is a humor columnist for *Senior Living* and *Eva Mag* and teaches humor writing workshops for the University of Tennessee and other organizations. A woman of small talents and big feet, Judy has published more than 100 humorous poems and essays.

Elsi Dodge is a single, retired special-education teacher whose RV trips across the continent span more than a quarter-century. She travels with Lady, her dog, and Dolphin, who thinks he's a saber-toothed tiger. Elsi's book, *RV Tourist: Tips, Tools, and Stories*, is available through her website: www.RVTourist.com.

Lindy B. Dolan lives in Niagara Falls, New York, where she and her husband are raising their three beautiful girls. In her spare time, Lindy makes inspirational name plaques, reads tons of books, and hangs with her friends and family. Please e-mail her at doltzoriginal@aol.com.

Lawrence D. Elliott is a nationally published author and has been an active Realtor in southern California since 1989. He lives in Ontario with his wife, Lisa, and his dog, Lacie. He also runs a network of real-estate websites, accessible through his main site at www.LawrenceElliott.com.

Debbie Farmer writes a weekly syndicated column.

John and **Carol Forrest** are retired from careers in education and health care. (respectively). They live in Orillia, Ontario, Canada, where they enjoy golfing, traveling, cruisin' in their classic '68 Mustang "ragtop," and following the life adventures of their grown children, Rob and Dana. They will celebrate their thirty-eighth anniversary in 2007.

Valerie J. Frost is a freelance writer and an office administrator at Horizon Christian Fellowship in San Diego, California. She and her husband, Terry, are parents of three grown children. They have thirteen energetic grandchildren, and two turbo-charged Jack Russell terriers named Rocket and Daphne.

Mark Geiger received his bachelor of science from the University of California, Riverside, in 1991. He owns his own business, LifeAfterCampus.com, where he sells two dating books he wrote and self-published. He would like to thank his lovely wife, Amy, for her inspiration and support. Contact Mark at geigerx2@pacbell.net.

Kerry Germain resides on the North Shore of Oahu, Hawaii, where she writes and publishes children's picture books. She's a fan of inspirational reading and enjoys telling stories—or, as they say in Hawaii, "talking story." Her newest picture book will be released in midsummer 2007. Visit her website at www.surfsupforkimo .com.

Loree Gold is a writer/producer for television and film. Her company, GoldPitt Films, Inc., produces educational and social awareness documentaries. Loree's also a professional songwriter and has been an NPR commentator. She lives in Nashville, Tennessee, and enjoys traveling, boxing, studying foreign languages, and living like there's no tomorrow.

Carol Sue Hahn received her M.Ed. from the University of Missouri. She has been a rehabilitation counselor and is now a special education professional. She enjoys hiking and traveling with her children, and her writing collection reflects the heart of her experiences.

Jeff S. Hamilton is a financial specialist living in Spruce Grove, Alberta. Besides spending much of his free time writing, he is also a collector of rare books and an avid traveler. Contact Jeff and read more of his essays at www.theduffzone .blogspot.com.

Bonnie Compton Hanson is the author of several books for adults and children, including the popular Ponytail Girls series, plus hundreds of articles and poems. She also speaks for Mothers of Preschoolers (MOPS), seniors, and women's and writing groups. Contact Bonnie at 3330 S. Lowell St., Santa Ana, CA 92707; bonnieh1@worldnet.att.net.

Jonny Hawkins dedicates the cartoons in this book to his sweet little baby, Kara Elise—a precious gift from God. His work can be seen in over 350 publications, in cartoon-a-day calendars, and in his latest book, *The Awesome Book of Healthy Humor.* He can be reached at jonnyhawkins2nz@yahoo.com. He lives with his wife, Carissa, two boys (Nate and Zach), and baby Kara in Sherwood, Michigan.

E. M. Hector is a lifelong creative writer. In high school, the National Council of Teachers of English chose her among 600 winners nationwide in their annual Achievement Award writing contest. Most of her writing, be it poetry, prose, or essay, has been inspired by her family. Her e-mail address is mywingdreams@ verizon.net.

Sheila S. Hudson is published in the Chicken Soup for the Soul series, the Chocolate for Women series, *God Allows U-Turns, Stories from the Heart* (Volumes 1 and 2), *Taking Education Higher,* and *God's Vitamin C.* Sheila is a travel columnist for *Athens Banner Herald,* contributor for several publications, and past president of the Southeastern Writers of America. She and her husband, Tim, are the proud grandparents of seven grandsons, known as the "magnificent seven." E-mail her at sheilahudson@charter.net.

Karen R. Kilby resides in Kingwood, Texas, with her husband, David. As a certified personality trainer with CLASServices, Inc., Karen enjoys helping people understand themselves and others through her seminars. Karen is also a regional speaker trainer and speaker for Stonecroft Ministries. Please reach her at krkilby@ kingwoodcable.net.

Betty King is the author of *It Takes Two Mountains to Make a Valley, but It Was in the Valleys I Grew, The Fragrance of Life,* and *In the Palm of His Hand.* She is a newspaper columnist of two weekly columns and a public speaker who lives with multiple sclerosis.

Emily King is the author of *Clopper the Christmas Donkey, Clopper and the Night Travelers* and *The Twiggenbotham Adventures*. She also contributed to *Chicken Soup for the Gardener's Soul*. Please visit Emily's website or contact her at www.emilyking.net or emily@emilyking.net.

Cheryl Kirking is an author, songwriter, and popular women's conference speaker who tickles the funny bones and tugs at the heartstrings of audiences nationwide. Her many books include the Christmas book with CD, *What Can I Give Jesus?* and her book for moms, *Crayons in the Dryer*. For booking information, visit www.cherylkirking.com.

Mimi Greenwood Knight is a freelance writer and artist living in what's left of south Louisiana with her husband, David, four kids, four dogs, four cats, and one obnoxious bird. Her parenting essays and articles have appeared in *Parents, American Baby, Working Mother, Christian Parenting Today, Today's Christian Woman,* and in anthologies including several Chicken Soup books.

Nancy Julien Kopp lives in the Flint Hills of Kansas. She writes fiction, essays, articles, and poetry. She has been published in newspapers, magazines, e-zines, and anthologies, including three *Chicken Soup for the Soul* books. She is a former teacher who still enjoys teaching through the written word.

Cheryl M. Kremer lives in Lancaster, Pennsylvania, with husband, Jack, and her two children, Nikki and Cobi. She works as a preschool teacher's aide and spends the rest of her time watching her children play field hockey, soccer, and basketball. She has been published in several other Chicken Soup books and can be reached at j_kremer@verizon.net.

William Livers is a school social worker with Southwest Parke Community Schools District in Montezuma, Indiana. He earned a master's degree in psychology from Southern Illinois University at Edwardsville, Illinois, and a master's degree in social work from Indiana University. William and his wife Tina have two children, Adam and Sarah. He enjoys spending time with his family and watching his kids do and say amazing things. He can be reached at blivers@swparke.k12.in.us.

Alice Malloy lives with her husband on Long Island, New York. Since her recent retirement, her new life consists of long walks by the ocean, spending time with her children and grandchildren, and writing a memoir about growing up in the fifties. Alice can be reached at aqmalloy@optonline.net.

Jennifer Martin is an author, speaker, television producer, and screenwriter living in Roseville, California. She gives workshops in writing for the metaphysical market and in Huna, the ancient tradition of the Hawaiian kahuna. You're invited to check out her website at www.hunawarrior.com or e-mail her at jenmartin@surewest.net.

Lisa May has enjoyed writing short stories and poems since she was young. She has had previous writings published in local and city papers, along with *Chicken Soup for the Latter-Day Saint Soul*. Her talent of expressing life in words, from pen to paper, has always been fascinating to her. She is the mother of two wonderful children and lives in the beautiful country of Temecula, California, with her husband, children, and yellow Lab, Lucky.

Dahlynn McKowen is the dedicated mother of two and a full-time author. She is an active coauthor for Chicken Soup for the Soul books and has created many titles, including *Fisherman's Soul, Entrepreneur's Soul, Soul in Menopause, Sisters' and Brothers' Soul* and the upcoming *Female Entrepreneur's Soul*. www.publishingsyndicate.com.

Sharon Melnicer is a writer, artist, and teacher in Winnipeg, Manitoba, Canada. She also frequently broadcasts the "slice-of-life" pieces that she pens on CBC local and national radio. A high-school English teacher on leave, she teaches "Lifestory Writing" to seniors for "Creative Retirement Manitoba." She is a busy, working artist who shows and sells throughout Canada and the United States.

Raymond L. Morehead, KTJ, FSA, Scotland. AA degree/Business Management with Highest Honors, Former USAF, Vietnam Veteran, father of three children and grandfather of seven, married thirty-seven years to his first and ony love. Raymond writes to inspire others and his grandchildren do the same. E-mail him at raymondHTJ@msn.com.

Brenda Nixon (www.brendanixon.com) is dedicated to building strong families through parent empowerment. She is the author of *Parenting Power in the Early Years,* a resource for parents/caregivers of young children, a contributing author to twenty books, and a popular speaker at family events.

Mark Parisi's "off the mark" comic panel has been syndicated since 1987 and is distributed by United Media. Mark's humor also graces greeting cards, T-shirts, calendars, magazines, newsletters, and books. Please visit his website at www.off themark.com. Lynn, his wife/business partner, and their daughter, Jen, contribute with inspiration (as do three cats).

Denise Peebles is from Rogersville, Alabama. She and her husband, Keith, have been married for twenty-four years. They have two children, Ashley and Jonathan. She has appeared in Chicken Soup several times and featured in magazines. Her dream is to publish a children's book. You can contact her at SPeeb47489@aol.com.

Christian novelist **Perry P. Perkins** was born and raised in Oregon. His writing includes *Just Past Oysterville* and *Shoalwater Voices.* Perry is a student of Jerry B. Jenkins Christian Writer's Guild and a frequent contributor to the Chicken Soup for the Soul anthologies. Perry's work can be found online at www.perryperkins books.com.

Teacher **Marilyn Phillips** is a cum laude graduate of Texas Woman's University. Her articles have appeared in *Guideposts, Living with Teenagers, Obadiah, Home Life,* and *Parent Life.* Contributed stories appear in six books, including *Chicken Soup for the Surviving Soul.* Marilyn has been married to Nolan since 1972 and has two children.

Stephanie Piro lives in New Hampshire (not too far from the beach!) with her husband, daughter, and three cats. She is one of King Features' team of women cartoonists, "Six Chix." (She is the Saturday chick!) Her single panel, "Fair Game," appears in newspapers and on her website: www.stephaniepiro.com. Her new book, *My Cat Loves Me Naked,* is available at bookstores everywhere. She also designs gift items for her company Strip Ts.

Barbara Puccia became a freelance writer after a twenty-year career in computers and education. She enjoys tennis and reading but spends most of her time dedicated to her children and volunteer work. Barbara is currently working on a series of humorous chapter books for early readers.

Kayleen Reusser has published more than 1,000 articles in dozens of publications, including *Chicken Soup for the Christian Soul 2, Today's Christian Woman, Decision, The Lookout,* and *Live.* She writes regularly for the travel and entertainment sections of a large metropolitan newspaper. Visit her website at www.KayleenR.com.

Phyllis Ring's work has appeared in the *Christian Science Monitor, Writer's Digest,* and *Yankee*. An instructor for the Long Ridge Writers Group, she taught English to kindergartners in China and served as program director at Green Acre Baha'i School in southern Maine. She can be reached at www.phyllisring.com.

Kimberly Ripley is a freelance writer and published author from Portsmouth, New Hampshire. A wife and mother of five, her days are filled with homeschooling her two teenagers and planning trips to Fort Myers, Florida. Kim is the author of *Freelancing Later in Life,* available online and through major bookstores.

Sallie A. Rodman is an award-winning author who loves to write about true inspirational moments in her life. She has contributed to many Chicken Soup anthologies, magazines, and the *Orange County Register*. She swears her three grown children, a husband, plus a cat and a dog, provide lots of writing ideas!

John E. Schlimm II is the author of several books, including *Corresponding with History, Straub Brewery, The Straub Beer Cookbook,* and *The Pennsylvania Celebrities Cookbook*. He earned his master's degree in education from Harvard University. He was born and raised in St. Marys, Pennsylvania. Please e-mail him at john schlimm@yahoo.com.

Tracy Schmid teaches first graders. After hours, she teaches multiaged students poetry. Tracy is a member of Ash Canyon Poets. She lives in Carson City, Nevada, with her two children and two dogs. She enjoys music, writing, theater, and a hot cup of black tea. Please email her at schmids@sbcglobal.net.

Michael Jordan Segal, who defied all odds after being shot in the head, is a husband, father, social worker, author, and inspirational speaker. His miraculous comeback story was first published in *Chicken Soup for the Christian Family Soul*. Since then, he's had numorous stories published. To contact Mike, please visit www.InspirationByMike.com or call 877-226-1003.

Dayle Allen Shockley's byline has appeared in dozens of publications. She is the author of three books and offers editorial services through her website at www.dayleshockley.com. Dayle lives in Texas with her husband and daughter. Please e-mail her at dayle@dayleshockley.com.

Robin Lee Shope is a language arts teacher and has had two dozen short stories published in popular collections such as Chicken Soup. Currently, her three novels are out in bookstores: *The Chase, The Replacement,* and *The Candidate*. Her next book, *Ruby Red and the Color of Home,* will be available through Amazon by Christmas 2007. You can e-mail her at write2robinshope@yahoo.com.

Jennifer Smith works with her husband at a boarding academy for at-risk teenagers. She is blessed to announce the arrival of her first children's book, *Things I Wonder*. Please visit www.hisworkpub.com to view the book and look for her upcoming book, *Rose, the Bubble-Breathing Dragon*.

Lizanne Southgate is an Oregon screenwriter and ghostwriter. She can be reached at lizannesghost@msn.com.

Ruth Spiro lives in Illinois with her husband and two daughters. Her articles and essays have appeared in *Child, Woman's World,* and *Family Fun,* as well as several anthologies. She is also the author of a children's book, *The Bubble Gum Artist*. She can be reached at www.ruthspiro.com.

Elva Stoelers is an award-winning Canadian writer. Most recently her work has appeared in *Chicken Soup for the New Mom's Soul, Chicken Soup for the Shopper's Soup,*

Chicken Soup for the Recovering Soul, and *Recovering Soul Daily Inspirations.* In addition to being broadcast on CBC Radio, she has been published internationally in a variety of small press parenting magazines.

Glorianne Swenson is a Minnesota-based published freelance writer and small business owner of Gloribks. Her genre includes creative nonfiction memoirs, devotionals, poetry, and children's picture book manuscripts. She is a wife, mother, and grandmother and enjoys singing, piano, geneology, photography, and antiquing. She may be e-mailed at gloribks@charter.net.

Kimberly Welsh, M.Ed., has been writing poems and stories since she was a child as gifts for family members and friends. She is a high-school English teacher. Kim loves to spend time with her husband and her two children. Her e-mail address is kimberlywelsh@esdnl.ca.

Ann Greenleaf Wirtz received a bachelor's in education from Bradley University and a master's from Illinois State. She has one son, was widowed, and remarried to Patrick, and authored *Sorrow Answered: A Journey of Grace.* She writes for the *Times-News* in North Carolina and is a hospice volunteer in Hendersonville, North Carolina. Write to her at annlouise1@bellsouth.net.

Helen Xenakis loves retirement living on Hilton Head. The lifestyle gives her plenty of time to pursue her interests, especially writing.

Pauline Youd is the author of children's Bible story books, magazine articles, and devotions for both adults and chidren. Her hobbies include musical comedy theater. Pauline teaches reading and Sunday school. She lives in California with her husband, Bill, and one very fluffy cat.

The Christmas Present. Reprinted by permission of Karen Rae Kilby. ©2006 Karen Rae Kilby.

Six Brown Eggs. Reprinted by permission of George H. Baty. ©1955 George H. Baty.

The Treasured Gifts Come Without Ribbons or Bows. Reprinted by permission of Cookie Curci. ©1989 Cookie Curci.

Papa's Radio. Reprinted by permission of Cookie Curci. ©1989 Cookie Curci.

Elvis Was Wrong! Reprinted by permission of Sallie A. Rodman. ©2006 Sallie A. Rodman.

A Christmas Moment. Reprinted by permission of Glorianne Marsyl Swenson. ©2002 Glorianne Marsyl Swenson.

Christmas Lost—and Found. Reprinted by permission of Catherine Michele Davis. ©2000 Catherine Michele Davis.

The Doll in Burgundy Twill. Reprinted by permission of Emily C. King. ©2005 Emily C. King.

God and Santa. Reprinted by permission of Elsi J. Dodge. ©2007 Elsi J. Dodge.

The Twelve Days of Christmas. Reprinted by permission of Janet Brennan. ©2001 Janet Brennan.

The Gift of Normandy Beach. Reprinted by permission of Sheila S. Hudson. ©2002 Sheila S. Hudson.

Caroling with the Coots. Reprinted by permission of Jennifer Noreen Martin. ©2006 Jennifer Noreen Martin.

Bearing Gifts. Reprinted by permission of Meredith Knight. ©2006 Meredith Knight.

Holiday Tale. Reprinted by permission of Michael Jordan Segal. ©2006 Michael Jordan Segal.

The World's Biggest Table. Reprinted by permission of Helen Xenakis. ©2007 Helen Xenakis.

All I Want for Christmas. Reprinted by permission of Alice Q. Malloy. ©2006 Alice Q. Malloy.

Milestones in the Boughs. Reprinted by permission of Dayle Allen Shockley. ©2005 Dayle Allen Shockley.

Taking Down the Christmas Tree. Reprinted by permission of Lyla Berry. ©2002 Lyla Berry.

Christmas Found. Reprinted by permission of Lisa May. ©2006 Lisa May.

Christmas Cards. Reprinted by permission of Deborah L. Farmer. ©2005 Deborah L. Farmer.

Paper Chains. Reprinted by permission of Tracy Schmid. ©2006 Tracy Schmid

The Christmas Bagel. Reprinted by permission of Barbara Puccia. ©2006 Barbara Puccia.

A Holiday to Remember. Reprinted by permission of Denise Peebles. ©2003 Denise Peebles

My Christmas Gift Shopping List

My Christmas Gift Shopping List

My Christmas Wish List

My Christmas Wish List

Celebrate the holidays

Code #3145 • $19.95

Code #0006 • $16.95

Code #0383 • $14.95

Also Available

Chicken Soup African American Soul
Chicken Soup African American Woman's Soul
Chicken Soup Breast Cancer Survivor's Soul
Chicken Soup Bride's Soul
Chicken Soup Caregiver's Soul
Chicken Soup Cat Lover's Soul
Chicken Soup Christian Family Soul
Chicken Soup College Soul
Chicken Soup Couple's Soul
Chicken Soup Dieter's Soul
Chicken Soup Dog Lover's Soul
Chicken Soup Entrepreneur's Soul
Chicken Soup Expectant Mother's Soul
Chicken Soup Father's Soul
Chicken Soup Fisherman's Soul
Chicken Soup Girlfriend's Soul
Chicken Soup Golden Soul
Chicken Soup Golfer's Soul, Vol. I, II
Chicken Soup Horse Lover's Soul, Vol. I, II
Chicken Soup Inspire a Woman's Soul
Chicken Soup Kid's Soul, Vol. I, II
Chicken Soup Mother's Soul, Vol. I, II
Chicken Soup Parent's Soul
Chicken Soup Pet Lover's Soul
Chicken Soup Preteen Soul, Vol. I, II
Chicken Soup Scrapbooker's Soul
Chicken Soup Sister's Soul, Vol. I, II
Chicken Soup Shopper's Soul
Chicken Soup Soul, Vol. I–VI
Chicken Soup at Work
Chicken Soup Sports Fan's Soul
Chicken Soup Teenage Soul, Vol. I–IV
Chicken Soup Woman's Soul, Vol. I, II

To order direct: Telephone (800) 441-5569 • www.hcibooks.com
Prices do not include shipping and handling. Your response code is CCS.

A CHICKEN SOUP FOR THE SOUL *Christmas*